S. HRG. 114–346

THE SECURITY AND POLITICAL CRISIS IN BURUNDI

HEARING

BEFORE THE

COMMITTEE ON FOREIGN RELATIONS UNITED STATES SENATE

ONE HUNDRED FOURTEENTH CONGRESS

FIRST SESSION

DECEMBER 9, 2015

Printed for the use of the Committee on Foreign Relations

Available via the World Wide Web: http://www.gpo.gov/fdsys/

U.S. GOVERNMENT PUBLISHING OFFICE

21–369 PDF WASHINGTON : 2016

For sale by the Superintendent of Documents, U.S. Government Publishing Office
Internet: bookstore.gpo.gov   Phone: toll free (866) 512–1800; DC area (202) 512–1800
Fax: (202) 512–2104   Mail: Stop IDCC, Washington, DC 20402–0001

(II)

CONTENTS

THE POLITICAL AND SECURITY CRISIS IN BURUNDI

Wednesday, December 9, 2015

U.S. SENATE
COMMITTEE ON FOREIGN RELATIONS SUBCOMMITTEE ON
AFRICA AND GLOBAL HEALTH POLICY
Washington, D.C.

The committee met, pursuant to notice, at 2:30 p.m., in Room SD–419, Dirksen Senate Office Building, Hon. Jeff Flake, chairman of the subcommittee, presiding.

Present: Senators Flake [presiding], Markey, Cardin, and Coons.

OPENING STATEMENT OF HON. JEFF FLAKE, U.S. SENATOR FROM ARIZONA

Senator FLAKE. This hearing of the Senate Foreign Relations Subcommittee on African and Global Health will come to order. I want to take a moment to thank our witnesses for arranging schedules to be here today and for your contribution to this hearing.

Today's hearing will focus on the political and security crisis in Burundi, where violence is increasing and instability is growing. Mass arrests, high-profile assassinations, and the killing of more than 200 people have caused at least 220,000 Burundians to flee the country.

President Nkurunziza's decision to run for a third term in office is widely viewed as a catalyst for this crisis, which has splintered his own party and hardened the line between his supporters and those who oppose him. But the roots of today's crisis precede the most recent elections in Burundi.

Today, we will examine Burundi's history, the Arusha Accords that ended its civil war, and how we can go back to the spirit of that agreement to end the conflict.

This particular part of the world has borne witness to many mass atrocities. Obviously, Burundi's 12-year civil war is among them. As we look to what has contributed to the breakdown of governance in Burundi today, it is important to pay attention to the ethnic underpinnings of this and previous conflicts.

Understanding the role that other actors in the region are playing is critical to understanding how to stop the violence in Burundi. I look forward to hearing from our witnesses on how the other actors are influencing the conflict there, perhaps for their own benefit, and what options are available to the United States to weigh in.

Unfortunately, President Nkurunziza is not the only leader of an African nation with the desire to hang on to his seat longer than is permitted. In the Great Lakes region alone, there are several elections coming up next year where the current leaders may well seek reelection through various means.

I look forward to hearing from our witnesses, hear what they think about the current crisis here, what it portends for these elections, and if we can expect similar outcomes from those who choose to stay in power longer. If so, how will these different crises intertwine? What will be the regional implications? And lastly, again, what should the United States be saying about these elections?

The bottom line is that the violence in Burundi needs to stop. The stakes are simply too high for these events to escalate.

With that, I will turn to recognize the ranking minority member on this committee, Senator Markey, for any comments you might have.

STATEMENT OF HON. EDWARD J. MARKEY, U.S. SENATOR FROM MASSACHUSETTS

Senator MARKEY. Thank you, Mr. Chairman. Thank you so much for having this very important and timely hearing. It is a critical moment for Burundi, the Great Lakes region of Africa, as well as for the wider African and international communities.

As President Obama said last July when Chairman Flake and I traveled with him to Africa, the continent's progress is impressive. It is one of the fastest growing regions in the world with a middle class projected to grow to more than 1 billion consumers. Africa is moving fast toward a better future, with millions reaching for opportunities that did not exist just a few years ago.

It is important to keep this larger picture in mind as we focus today on Burundi, a country that has experienced deep political division and escalating political violence since last spring.

Since the Arusha Accords ended Burundi's civil war in 1993, the country has continued to face challenges, but its politics have been relatively free of violence. While the international community and the United Nations have played a critical role in this process, all of the credit for the advances up until last spring rightly go to the Burundian people and its leaders in government, opposition, and civil society, who consciously worked toward national harmony.

With the political turmoil that began last spring, it has become apparent that the work of over 20 years could come undone unless all of the leaders of Burundi take seriously their solemn duty to find common ground, to seriously negotiate ways to accommodate one another's legitimate interests, and to guarantee that the security and fundamental rights of all of Burundi's people are protected.

The people of Burundi have suffered enough. A grinding poverty is accompanied by ongoing turmoil, including mass arrests, several high-profile assassinations, and over 200 reported extrajudicial killings since April. At least 210,000 Burundians have now fled into neighboring countries. An armed conflict in Burundi could draw in neighboring countries and non-state actors elsewhere in the conflict-torn Great Lakes region. The consequences in terms of Burundi and the region could be devastating.

We are committed to helping Burundi change course, to turn away from violence, and for political rivals to sincerely negotiate with each other and make common cause for the good of all of the people of Burundi. That is why this hearing is so important.

And I thank you, Mr. Chairman, for calling for it. We very much appreciate the witnesses' willingness to join us today, and I look forward to hearing your testimony.

Thank you, Mr. Chairman.

Senator FLAKE. Thank you, Senator Markey.

The only witness in this first panel is Assistant Secretary Thomas-Greenfield.

Thank you for being here. We know that you are busy. We know how much you travel to the region and the time you put in. We appreciate you being here. Obviously, your entire comments will be made a part of the record. Please, if you can keep it close to 5 minutes, we will have time and have the next panel as well. We look forward to your testimony.

Assistant Secretary?

STATEMENT OF HON. LINDA THOMAS–GREENFIELD, ASSISTANT SECRETARY, BUREAU OF AFRICAN AFFAIRS, U.S. DEPARTMENT OF STATE, WASHINGTON, D.C.

Ms. THOMAS-GREENFIELD. Thank you very much, Chairman Flake and Ranking Member Markey, for the opportunity to testify before you today on Burundi.

As you noted, the situation in Burundi is very worrisome, and the stakes are very high. The Department of State and the Bureau of African Affairs, in particular, greatly appreciate the bipartisan support we continue to receive for our work, our Embassies, and our people, who spend every day striving to promote U.S. national security, foreign policy, and economic interests on the African continent.

In Central Africa, we have focused on our core values: strengthening democratic institutions, spurring economic growth, advancing peace and security, and promoting opportunity and development.

Occupying significant attention over the past year, however, is Burundi. Burundi has sadly become a cautionary tale for the region about how a leader who will do anything to stay in power can undermine a decade of peace and post-conflict reconciliation.

President Nkurunziza's pursuit of non-inclusive, nonconsensual elections, as characterized by the African Union's October 17 communique, sparked the current crisis. His decision also clearly violated terms of the 2000 Arusha agreement that led to the end of the Burundian civil war and became the country's foundation for governance, peace, and security.

Since the discredited elections last summer, the crisis in Burundi has worsened, with Nkurunziza in isolation and his government taking an increasingly hard line against any form of perceived opposition or critique, even from within the ruling party ranks.

A daily pattern of retaliatory attacks between security forces and armed elements of the opposition has continued for months. The repression and violence has forced over 220,000 Burundians to flee the country over the last 8 months, and the U.N. Office of the High Commissioner of Refugees has documented at least 240 killings of individuals in Burundi in the same time frame.

In response to these troubling events, we have pursued an aggressive three-pronged strategy to prevent mass violence.

First, we are directing pressure at the Government of Burundi and armed opposition to step back from increasingly violent actions as well as rhetoric.

Second, we are accelerating the launch of a credible dialogue process under African leadership to find a political solution.

Third, we are reaching out to the region and international community to encourage their support while supporting regional contingency planning by the A.U. in case the violence worsens.

We believe that our pressure on and direct engagement with the Government of Burundi and with opposition leaders, as well as our broader outreach to the region and international community, has positively impacted the situation. It has done so both by helping to stave off what we feared could have been wider spread violence and by providing a window to press for regional efforts to support a political solution through internationally mediated dialogue. But that window cannot last indefinitely.

The underlying calculus of those in the government that they will use all means necessary to retain power has not changed. In addition to our suspension of in-country training support for Burundian military and law enforcement, and the withdrawal of AGOA trade benefits effective January 2016, President Obama issued an executive order on November 23 imposing economic sanctions and a travel ban on four individuals, two from the government side and two of the May coup plotters.

The implementation of a sanctions regime underscores the seriousness with which we view the severity of the crisis and demonstrates the President's commitment to using all the tools available to discourage violence and encourage a political resolution. We will not hesitate to add additional individuals to the list.

We are in daily contact with members of the Burundi Government and opposition, as well as regional leaders. Our senior leaders, including President Obama as well as Secretary Kerry, have engaged with stakeholders in Burundi and throughout the region with a topline message to refrain from violence and pursue dialogue.

In November, President Obama delivered a video message directly to the Burundian people, in which he called on all the country leaders to seek a peaceful solution for the country through dialogue. This was very well-received in Burundi.

Special Envoy Perriello has spent the bulk of the past 3 months in the region and in Europe, including an emergency deployment to Burundi to deter the launch of the government's planned security operation in early November, which we feared could have instigated much more widespread violence.

Ambassador Liberi and our Embassy staff worked around the clock under intense circumstances to maintain crucial lines of communication and provide a voice for peace and human rights.

We cannot afford further delay of the dialogue process without risking an escalation in repression and violence. With the process currently entrusted to Ugandan President Museveni on behalf of the East African Community, we continue to hope to see dialogue initiated in the very near future. If it is not, and the crisis deteriorates further, possibly into full-scale war, I fear that President Museveni and the EAC could end up being partially blamed, given the lengthy delays in getting a process started.

We have encouraged the EAC leaders, as well as those in the broader region, to support peace and dialogue, and to ensure that this crisis does not become another protracted regional conflict dominating the continent's time and resources. We strongly support the commencement of dialogue, active A.U. leadership, and the need for a full-time mediator.

At the same time, other regional leaders are contemplating efforts to extend their own terms in office beyond constitutional limits. President Obama articulated the U.S. position very clearly in Addis Ababa when you both were there in July when he said that Africa's democratic progress is put at risk when leaders refuse to step aside at the end of their terms.

Leaders who try to change the rules to stay in power solely for personal gain risk instability and strife in their countries. We are seeing this play out in Burundi and the Republic of Congo as well as elsewhere.

Our policy position enjoys overwhelming support across Africa. This is in the words of Secretary Kerry a decisive moment for democracy in Africa. The steps that we take now to encourage peaceful transitions of power may encourage other leaders in the region from following Burundi's path and encourage them to make the right decision for their countries and their people.

Senator Flake, Ranking Member Markey, and members of the subcommittee, I want to thank you again for holding this hearing and giving us the opportunity to brief you on the situation in Burundi. I hope the information is useful to the subcommittee. I have submitted a much longer version of my testimony for the record, and I am happy to answer your questions.

[The prepared statement of Ms. Thomas-Greenfield follows:]

PREPARED STATEMENT OF ASSISTANT SECRETARY LINDA THOMAS-GREENFIELD

Thank you very much Chairman Flake, Ranking Member Markey, and other Members of the Committee for the opportunity to testify today on the many challenges facing Burundi.

The Department of State and the Bureau of African Affairs in particular greatly appreciate the bipartisan support we continue to receive for our work, our embassies, and our people who spend every day striving to promote U.S. national security, foreign policy, and economic interests on the African continent.

In Central Africa, we have focused on strengthening democratic institutions, spurring economic growth, advancing peace and security, and promoting opportunity and development. Occupying significant attention over the past year, Burundi has sadly become a cautionary tale for the region about how a leader who will do anything to stay in power can undermine a decade of peace and post-conflict reconciliation.

The current crisis in Burundi began more than a year ago when the Burundian government began an increasingly repressive crackdown against journalists, civil society, and all political opponents. In the months leading up to his decision in April 2015 to stand for a third presidential term in Burundi President Pierre Nkurunziza's government was responsible for increasingly harsh repression, intimidation, and violence towards legitimate political opposition, independent media, and anyone within his own party who dissented against this plan. Credible local and international human rights groups have documented a harrowing number of cases of torture and extra-judicial killings over the past two years. Nkurunziza's pursuit of "non-inclusive, non-consensual elections"—as characterized by the African Union's October 17th communique—after a decade of irresponsible governance and failure to alleviate poverty in Burundi—sparked the current crisis. His decision to pursue a third term also clearly violated terms of the 2000 Arusha Agreement which led to the end of the Burundian Civil War and became the foundation for relative peace and security over the past decade. Furthermore, the presidential elections, held in late July, were widely viewed as not credible, not fair, not free, and not transparent.

Since the election, we have seen the crisis in Burundi only worsen—with the Nkurunziza government taking an increasingly hard line against any form of perceived opposition or critique, even if it comes from within the ruling party's ranks. The crisis has for months been characterized by a daily pattern of retaliatory attacks between security forces and armed elements of the opposition or those perceived to be opponents of the ruling party. More recently, this has included beheading and disembowelment of victims. The UN Office of the High Commissioner for Human Rights (OHCHR) has documented at least 240 killings of individuals in Burundi since April. Members of the ruling party, including public security forces, have used extreme violence with impunity and targeted the most vulnerable members of the country's population, namely those trying to flee the country as refugees. The government has not taken action to seriously investigate credible allegations of human rights violations and abuses by members of the ruling party youth wing, known as the Imbonerakure, the Burundian National Police, and the National Intelligence Service, nor has the government taken action to hold these same groups accountable.

The repression and violence have forced over 220,000 Burundians to flee into neighboring countries since April, when Nkurunziza announced his decision to pursue a third term. Many of those attempting to flee have reported violent confrontations by party militias and police while en route. Since the crisis began in April 2015, amorphous groups of armed opposition actors have also carried out violence against the security services and key targets in Bujumbura, and in Burundi's border areas, further exacerbating the conflict.

Inflammatory rhetoric used by President Nkurunziza and the Senate President threatening a disarmament operation in November stoked fears of greater violence throughout the country. I will discuss this later, but we firmly believe that the consequent outpouring of international messaging and pressure prevented the November 8th ultimatum from being the start of wider-spread violence.

At the same time, some elements opposed to President Nkurunziza have conducted targeted attacks on government officials, police officers, and civilians. These actions also threaten to escalate the situation and spark more widespread violence. While Nkurunziza's cynical attempts to treat all of those opposed to his actions as coup plotters must be rejected, it is equally important for those opposition members who have taken up arms to renounce violence and fully commit themselves to reaching a political consensus for the way forward.

As this crisis has unfolded, we have been actively engaged with Burundian and regional stakeholders, donor partners, and other allies in preventing Burundi from returning to war. We believe that our direct engagement with the Government of Burundi and opposition members, as well as our broader outreach to the region and international community, has impacted the situation by helping to hold off widerspread violence and giving us a window to support regional efforts to find a political solution through internationally-mediated dialogue. But that window of time will not last indefinitely. The underlying calculus of the government - that it will use all means necessary to retain power—has not changed.

Since the discredited election and an increase in violence, we have pursued an aggressive three-pronged strategy to prevent mass violence by: 1) directing pressure at the Government of Burundi and armed opposition to step back from increasingly violent action; 2) accelerating the launch of credible peace talks under African leadership to find a political solution; and 3) supporting regional contingency planning by the AU in case violence worsens.

We are in daily contact with the Burundian government and opposition, and regional leaders. Our senior leaders, including President Obama, Ambassador Rice, Secretary Kerry, Ambassador Power, Assistant Secretary Malinowski, and I have called or met with stakeholders throughout Burundi and the region with the top line message to refrain from violence and to pursue dialogue. For example, earlier in November, President Obama delivered a video message directly to the Burundian people calling on the country's leaders to seek a peaceful solution for the country through dialogue. The video was very well received by the region, specifically the appeal to all for non-violence and the recognition of the military's professionalism and restraint thus far. President Obama has also reached out to regional leaders such as South African President Zuma to call for calm and press for a dialogue that can bring about a long-term solution to the crisis. Special Envoy Perriello has spent the bulk of the past three months in the region and Europe, including emergency deployment to Burundi to deter the launch of Operation Kora, a government-planned public disarmament campaign, in early November. Ambassador Liberi and our Embassy staff have worked around the clock under intense circumstances to maintain crucial lines of communication and provide a voice for peace and human rights.

Since the beginning of the electoral cycle, we have called on Burundians and regional actors to play constructive roles and to reject violence before, during, and after the presidential elections. Our messaging has targeted the government and its supporters for unlawful violence against peaceful protestors, the participants in the attempted illegal seizure of power last May, and any others who have sought or are seeking to use violence to advance their agenda.

We have also joined our donor partners in increasing the costs for the regime and armed opposition for the use of repression and violence. We suspended in-country delivery of the Train and Equip mission of our Africa Contingency Operations Training and Assistance peacekeeping program as well as provision of assistance under the African Military Education Program. We also suspended International Law Enforcement Academy and Anti-Terrorism Assistance training that had been provided to Burundian law enforcement agencies. In early November we announced that AGOA trade preference benefits will be withdrawn from Burundi effective January 1, 2016.

More recently, President Obama announced an Executive Order on November 23rd, imposing economic sanctions and a travel ban on four individuals, two officials within the government and two of the May coup plotters. The establishment of a sanctions regime underscores the severity of the crisis and the President's commitment to using all tools available to pressure Burundian stakeholders to resist violence and seek a political resolution. With the sanctions regime in place, we will not hesitate to add additional individuals to the list, including those aiding and abetting individuals already sanctioned. We continue to assess whether to designate additional individuals or entities for sanction under the Executive Order.

It heartens me to see the Burundian people continue to reject attempts to turn the ongoing political crisis into an ethnic conflict. This crisis is first and foremost a political one, driven by a break within the ruling party over Nkurunziza's insistence in staying in power. While we remain vigilant about any attempt to turn this crisis into an ethnic conflict, it is important to remember that until the advent of this crisis, Burundi was considered a success story in overcoming ethnic division. The integration of the military and civil society are models of post-conflict reconciliation, and have remained a strong, but fraying bulwark against efforts to divide and inflame. The outcome of this crisis will determine whether the youth in Burundi, which make up the majority of the population, remain a relatively post-ethnic generation, or whether ethnic and political divides are locked in for more decades.

The best route for resolving this crisis remains an internationally-mediated dialogue amongst all Burundian stakeholders that is hosted outside of Burundi so all stakeholders can safely attend. Members of the East African Community (EAC) entrusted Ugandan President Museveni back in July to facilitate such a dialogue, and our top diplomatic priority is accelerating the start of this process, whether in Kampala, Addis, or Arusha. Each day without credible peace talks is read as a permission slip for the government or the opposition to escalate repression and violence. We simply cannot afford further delay, and that is our top message to the region. If war breaks out before the dialogue starts, the EAC could end up being partially blamed for the delay in starting a dialogue.

The very existence of talks, even if they falter, would release pressure and give the international community and the region a focal point for diplomatic pressure on all sides. We continue to reach out to President Museveni, the African Union, and other EAC leaders to press them to immediately convene a dialogue. We have made known that we are ready to support the dialogue, including through the international team of envoys as observers. We strongly support active AU leadership and the need for a full-time mediator.

While we continue to strive for a political solution, we are urging our UN and AU partners to undertake contingency planning for the worst case scenario. We believe the best and most viable option would be an AU-mandated regional force, possibly with the East African Standby Force. We are in regular contact with the AU and made clear our readiness to help should the situation call for regional, multi-lateral intervention.

We continue to be seized by this crisis, and are working with the EAC, AU, EU, UN and others. Special Envoy Perriello plans to join the EU, AU and UN Envoys for the Great Lakes Region of Africa for a visit to Burundi and its neighbors later this month, as well as to Addis and Kampala to press the urgency of talks.

Despite our best efforts, we recognize that more must be done to ensure that Burundi can exit the path of violence and shift toward a peaceful settlement of the political crisis. The international community remains engaged, and we have been active in New York, Geneva, and bilaterally to keep Burundi on the international agenda. The UN Security Council is considering a visit to Burundi early in the new year. The Pope appealed for peace in Burundi during his recent visit to Africa. We will continue to encourage international pressure and visibility on the Burundi crisis so that all the interlocutors fully understand the stakes.

The crisis in Burundi has also beset its neighbors with refugees continuing to cross into Tanzania, Rwanda, Uganda, and the DRC, and at times exacerbated existing regional tensions. We have encouraged all of the EAC's leaders and the broader region to support peace and dialogue and ensure this crisis does not become another protracted regional conflict that dominates the continent's time and resources.

At the same time, other regional leaders themselves are contemplating efforts to extend their own terms in office beyond constitutional limits. President Obama articulated the U.S. position on this very clearly in Addis Ababa in July when he said that Africa's democratic progress is put at risk when leaders refuse to step aside at the end of their terms. He added that leaders who try to change the rules to stay in power solely for personal gain risk instability and strife in their countries, and we are seeing this play out in Burundi, in the Republic of the Congo, where a referendum was just held on a new constitution that would allow President Sassou N'guesso to run again by doing away with term limits provisions, and elsewhere. Our policy position enjoys overwhelming support across Africa, particularly from its youth.

We have engaged directly with the presidents of this region approaching elections with that very same message. As Secretary Kerry wrote in an October 6 op-ed, this is a decisive moment for democracy in Africa. While each situation and each country context is unique, the steps that we take now to encourage peaceful transitions may help to prevent similar crises from occurring. The Burundi crisis is a cautionary tale for others in the region. No leader wants to be in Nkurunziza's situation, fearing for his life, watching his nation's economy plummet and his citizens flee the country. Others in the region still have an opportunity to avoid Burundi's path and make the right decision for their country and their people.

Senator Flake, Ranking Member Markey, and Members of the subcommittee, thank you again for holding this hearing and giving me the opportunity to brief you on the steps we are taking to address the situation in Burundi. I hope this information is helpful to the subcommittee. I am glad to answer any questions you might have.

Senator FLAKE. Well, thank you. I really appreciate this.

As you know, some of the coalition of opposition leaders there have made it clear that no peace will be possible as long as Nkurunziza remains in power. He is committed and has no intention, it seems, of stepping down.

What is going to give? First, is this just a "who blinks" here? Or is there going to be pressure from the EAC and others to break the logjam?

Ms. THOMAS-GREENFIELD. We are trying every way to encourage all of the regional partners to put pressure on President Nkurunziza as well as the opposition to go to the negotiating table to start a dialogue process.

The EAC's early attempts did not work. They have turned the process over to President Museveni. Right now, our Special Envoy Perriello is in Uganda and hoping to encourage the Ugandans to step up their efforts in pushing for and starting the dialogue.

But we are also putting pressure on the A.U. We have had a number of conversations with the A.U. In fact, the A.U. deployed a special envoy or a representative of the A.U. chairperson. That is President Boni Yayi of Benin. He was sent to Burundi yesterday. Unfortunately, his plane was not allowed to land. But their efforts will continue. We are hopeful that eventually we will get someone in.

It is important that President Nkurunziza meet with the parties and start this process so that we can see some solution to what is happening there.

Senator FLAKE. I would assume it is a little difficult for somebody like Museveni, who has been there since 1986 and is planning to run again, to speak with much credibility about leaving after the two terms that that Arusha Accords spells out.

You talked about some of the sanctions we imposed on individuals, travel sanctions, other suspensions of other programs that we have. What additional leverage do we have, as far as the U.S. goes?

Ms. THOMAS-GREENFIELD. I think we can impose additional sanctions to the ones that we have already imposed. We also have additional leverage as it relates to other partners. We are working closely with the EU. They have just concluded what they refer to as Article 96 negotiations with the government. They were key contributors to budgetary support for the Burundi Government.

Those discussions with the EU did not go well, which leads to the next step, which would be their ending their support for the government. We are working very closely with them as they move forward on those efforts, as well as supporting efforts to impose additional sanctions on additional individuals.

Senator FLAKE. There are in the region other actors there and other influences on this. There have been reports that the Rwandan Government is secretly recruiting an army of Burundian refugees, presumably for the purpose of conducting some kind of armed insurgency inside Burundi.

There was a letter to the editor in the Washington Post in November, written by Jeff Drumtra, a former U.N. official, who outlined what he saw there in those camps. If these reports are true, what is the State Department doing to press the Rwandan Government from doing this, from stepping up recruiting efforts like this, or to stop these recruiting efforts?

Ms. THOMAS-GREENFIELD. Sir, we have seen these reports, and we have had a number of conversations with the Rwandan Government to encourage them to investigate the reports. Any efforts that are being made within refugee camps on the borders of Rwanda should be stopped.

We are encouraging the Rwandans as well to be more proactive in supporting the peace process. We have also had discussions with them to discourage any actions being taken by the Rwandan Government to support additional violence that might take place in the region.

Senator FLAKE. Do you put stock in those reports yourself?

Ms. THOMAS-GREENFIELD. I have seen reports coming from UNHCR. We work closely with UNHCR, and I trust that if they are reporting this, they have seen the basis for making these reports and allegations.

Senator FLAKE. Let us talk about the DRC for a minute. What pressures are coming from the DRC?

Ms. THOMAS-GREENFIELD. Again, additionally, we have had conversations with President Kabila over the past 2 years and probably even longer to discuss with him his efforts to change the constitution so that he might seek a third term.

Fortunately, the constitution does not allow that change in DRC. I continue to be hopeful that he will make the right decision and not run for a third term and keep the country moving in the right direction and not turn back the very meager democratic gains that they have made over the past 10 years.

Our special envoy has as well been to DRC on a number of occasions. Secretary Kerry was there last year as well. We continue to have conversations with the President on this issue.

Senator FLAKE. What kind of border pressures and issues are there with the DRC?

Ms. THOMAS-GREENFIELD. I am sorry?

Senator FLAKE. What kind of border pressures are there? With Rwanda, you have refugees going across and allegedly being used by the Rwandan Government. What are we seeing in terms of refugees?

Ms. THOMAS-GREENFIELD. We are seeing refugees cross into all of Burundi's neighbors. In addition to Rwanda, Tanzania has more than 50,000 refugees. DRC has a large number of refugees, as well as Uganda.

Also, in the case of DRC, there are armed groups that are based in DRC. Some fear that those groups might participate in the violence in that country. So it is a very volatile situation along that border.

Senator FLAKE. Some were surprised that Nkurunziza, when he was outside the country and there was a coup staged, that he was able to maintain or regain control when he returned.

Is he in a stronger position now? If he is, is it just because the opposition is splintered so much?

Ms. THOMAS-GREENFIELD. You know, we regret that coup taking place. We do not support those kinds of actions, and we have made that very clear. But I do not believe the president is in a stronger position. I think because of the decision to seek a third term, he has weakened his position significantly, both within his party as well as outside his party.

The information that we are getting from inside of Burundi is that he is in isolation. He is not in the capital. I do not think when he made the decision to run for a third term that he thought he was going to be president of a country that was imploding. That implosion is a result of his decision.

Senator FLAKE. Senator Markey?

Senator MARKEY. Thank you.

Thank you for all your good work on this issue.

So the President of Uganda is the mediator, but he has his own tough election next year, so he is going to be distracted in terms of his role. That creates a problem, a political distraction, when we need something that is real and now, an intervention with some passion and immediacy to solve the problem.

Should the U.N., in your opinion, send in Chapter VII peacekeepers at this time, in order to help keep the peace?

Ms. THOMAS-GREENFIELD. President Museveni is engaged in his election, and I think very much distracted from the process. I think when he took on this responsibility from the Tanzanians, he hoped that it could be resolved quickly.

He has assigned his minister of defense to oversee the negotiations. Again, they have not, as of yet, bore any fruit.

Senator MARKEY. Again, that is a lot different than the president of a country.

Ms. THOMAS-GREENFIELD. Yes. He actually traveled there himself.

Senator MARKEY. I know, but over the next several months here——

Ms. THOMAS-GREENFIELD. We are hopeful that in this process the A.U. will become more actively engaged in the negotiations and take this burden away from President Museveni.

Senator MARKEY. What is Zuma saying to us?

Ms. THOMAS-GREENFIELD. She is very engaged, as I mentioned earlier. She just deployed her own special representative, President Boni Yayi, to Burundi. We have not had an opportunity to speak to him about what his tasks are, but we saw that as a positive sign.

Senator MARKEY. The Hutu are organizing along ethnic lines and militarizing along ethnic lines, and that is always kind of a prelude to a failed state. So can you talk a little bit about that and this division that is developing more along arms lines between the Hutu and the Tutsi and how that ethnic traditional rivalry is now affecting the politics and the difficulty in finding a political resolution?

Ms. THOMAS-GREENFIELD. You know, Senator, actually we are buoyed by the fact that the ethnic part of this conflict has not taken root yet. It is a concern, but——

Senator MARKEY. Do you see militarization developing along ethnic lines?

Ms. THOMAS-GREENFIELD. There is some militarization developing, but it is also within the ranks of the Hutu, as well as among the Tutsis, but I do not think the divisions are as sharp yet as they might become. We are worried about that happening, but at this point, that has not happened. I think the military has particularly avoided that.

Again, we are seeing conflict within the Hutu ranks, within the president's party. So this is not yet one that has divided along those two fissures, which I think would be a really serious step in the wrong direction.

Senator MARKEY. What is your view about the suitability of the East African Community to be able to deal with a problem of this magnitude? Is that really within their capacity to respond in a way that is going to avoid a civil war?

Ms. THOMAS-GREENFIELD. It could be in their capacity. They have not been able to successfully achieve that because there are tensions within the EAC as it relates to Burundi. There are tensions, clearly, between Burundi and Rwanda, but also tensions between Rwanda and Tanzania.

Those tensions have caused the EAC not to be as effective as they might have been. For that reason, we do think having the A.U. take on this role would be a good thing.

Senator MARKEY. Does that point more toward a U.N. Chapter VII peacekeeping mission?

Ms. THOMAS-GREENFIELD. I do not think we have reached that point yet. We have been in discussion with the A.U. about moving forward on contingency planning, so that if there is a need for a protection force in Burundi, that the A.U. would be able to pull that together very, very quickly.

We have also been in discussion with the U.N. about the possibilities of using troops out of DRC who are along the border to provide protection. The Chapter VII discussions have not taken place yet.

Senator MARKEY. Tell us a little bit, if you could, about your targeted measures against individuals in the country and who you are talking about and what those measures might be.

Ms. THOMAS-GREENFIELD. We have designated four individuals thus far for targeted sanctions. It was two from the government side and two who were involved in the failed coup plot. We are looking at individuals who have been responsible for exacerbating the instability in Burundi, who have contributed to the violence, and who are standing in the way of peace.

So, again, there are two right now on the government side and two on the opposition side.

Senator MARKEY. Okay, thank you.

Ms. THOMAS-GREENFIELD. And we are looking at others as well.

Senator MARKEY. I think, from my perspective, as I look at this, in the absence of actual regional forces stepping up to deal with this issue, I think it should telescope the time frame that it takes for the U.N. to consider an active peacekeeping intervention. If we are waiting for all these countries on the sidelines to finally get their act together, it may be too late, and the ethnic divisions become so strong that putting the country back together again becomes very difficult.

So I would recommend that you look at that and just make a clear-eyed judgment as to whether or not they are going to be able to resolve their own political differences in the surrounding countries. If not, I think we have to ask the U.N. to act.

Ms. THOMAS-GREENFIELD. There are discussions and plans for a Security Council trip to Burundi early next year, and I think that as well as many other issues will be on their plate to consider.

Senator MARKEY. So I just think it is pretty clear that the President of Uganda is distracted, the other countries have their own political considerations, and meanwhile in the middle here is a president who is not really as concerned with the overall long-term historical well-being of his country. I just think we have a big role that we can play in the intervention.

The sooner we make the intervention, the sooner everyone else is going to have to pay attention as well. I think this is a problem Africa should be solving. I think the sooner we get in, the sooner they will say, "We are going to solve it for you. We should take this role." But I think it has to happen soon.

Thank you so much for all your great work.

Ms. THOMAS-GREENFIELD. Thank you, sir.

Senator FLAKE. Senator Coons?

Senator COONS. Thank you, Chairman Flake and Ranking Member Markey, for holding this hearing that I think is so important.

Thank you and great to see again, Assistant Secretary. Thank you for your tireless and dedicated work and your focus on this issue.

The United States and the world are watching what is happening in Burundi. Back in August, I had the opportunity to lead a bipartisan codel to Rwanda, where we visited the memorial to the victims of genocide of 1994.

Members of this Congress are committed to not letting such a stain on humanity happen again. So we are eager to work with you and the administration to make sure we are deploying all the capabilities and resources of the U.S. Government to meaningfully engage with this.

The Burundian Government and the opposition must pursue a negotiated peace process, as you said in your testimony. Each day without credible peace talks is being read as a permission slip for the government or the opposition to escalate repression or violence. We cannot let that happen.

There needs to be accountability for those who have been fomenting violence.

As you discussed, what is happening in Burundi is also important because it can affect the future of other countries in the region, not the least of which is the DRC, as they prepare for their elections. It is my hope that President Kabila takes appropriate lessons from what is happening in Burundi and that he should not aspire to mire his country in even greater conflict by going down the ill-conceived path of President Nkurunziza.

Regional leaders like Ugandan President Museveni have a critical role to play. Regional structures like the East African Community and the A.U. do.

Our President Barack Obama has spoken of African solutions to African problems. When it comes to security and political crises like the ones we are seeing in Burundi, regional leaders need to partner with the international community and with us to develop meaningful solutions.

So I am grateful for your focus on this, Mr. Chairman, and for your leadership.

Tell me, if you would, just answers to three brief questions.

What greater role can Congress play in preventing mass atrocities, specifically in Burundi but also elsewhere around the world? I know Senator Cardin is working on the mass atrocity board authorization bill. I would be interested in your view on what Congress can do here in Burundi as well as around the world.

Second, just tell us a little more, if you would, about our efforts to support contingency planning by the U.N., by the A.U., by the EAC.

And tell me, if you would, under what conditions you would seek additional authorities or funding from Congress for either stabilization assistance or humanitarian assistance relative to Burundi. Thank you.

Ms. THOMAS-GREENFIELD. Thank you, Senator, and it is great to see you. And again, thank you for everything that that you are doing to support our efforts.

In terms of the role of Congress, there are a number of things you can do, particularly these kinds of hearings give a tremendous amount of highlight to this issue, both here in Washington but also in Africa. It amazes me the extent to which I hear from Africans what I say and what you say in these hearings. They need to know that our Congress, our Senate, is engaged on this issue.

So that is the first thing, and you are already doing it, and it really does make a huge difference.

The kinds of trips that you have taken to Rwanda and delivering the tough messages so that countries know that there is no light between the Congress and the administration on this issue are important. They need to hear from you on a regular basis that you support the efforts, you support the policy, and you are demanding the change.

I sometimes use you when I am in meetings with heads of state. "If I do not do this, my Congress is going to be on my head. You need to make a difference because it is not just me saying this but the entire U.S. Government, including our Congress, is a part of the process."

So having a strong, unified message from the Senate to President Nkurunziza—he looks for divisions within us. Those divisions are used. So having that message delivered to him in no uncertain terms, or any of these heads of state in the region, I think again gets the message across in a strong way.

In terms of contingency planning, we were very pleased to hear from the A.U. that they have now intensified their contingency-planning efforts. We have been in conversation with them for probably the last 8 months to push contingency planning forward. We have offered some of our planners to support their effort. That offer is still on the table. They are moving forward with this, as well as having conversations with the East African standby force.

The important element of putting together a contingency plan is what troops will be used and to make sure that we have troops that have the support of both sides, and who are not seen to be taking sides.

So it is really important that we encourage some of the countries who are outside of the region, the immediate region, to participate in any troop deployments that we make in the region.

The EC has indicated their support for this effort. We are in constant conversation with the EU.

In fact, the five envoys—the EU envoy, our envoy, A.U., U.N., and the Belgium envoy—are traveling together in the region right now and are putting together a very strong front to respond to this.

In terms of funding, of course, the humanitarian side is huge. The humanitarian impact of what is happening in Burundi cannot go unnoticed. Two-hundred-twenty-thousand refugees is not a small number.

When we start looking at those numbers in Europe, we think they are huge. They are huge in Africa as well.

We need to be able to provide the support to refugees and respond to the humanitarian crisis that is coming out of this with robust funding. And the U.S. Government's funding has been critical to support refugees.

But we also have to look at what we do on building the capacity of civil society, as well as governments, to build strong governance. We have worked closely with civil society and even the parties in Burundi in the early days. But certainly, we had limited resources in that area. We need to do more. We need to do more to support good governance and build institutions that are strong and that people have confidence in.

We see when we do that it works. It has worked in Burundi. It has worked in Nigeria. It has worked in Cote d'Ivoire. And it can work in Central Africa, with the right amount of resources to put into play.

Senator COONS. Terrific, thank you, Madam Assistant Secretary. Thank you, Mr. Chairman.

Senator FLAKE. Thank you.

Senator Markey brought up the prospect of this devolving into some kind of ethnic conflict like we have seen in that area, obviously, before. You mentioned that, gratefully, it is not there.

What are the warning signs that we are looking for? Where is the tipping point there when it becomes an ethnic conflict? What should we be looking for there?

Ms. THOMAS-GREENFIELD. We have seen some warning signs already. Several weeks ago, the language coming out of the president and the president of the senate were very alarmist. They were using references that we saw used prior to the start of the genocide in Rwanda.

We pulled out all the stops during a very short period of time to highlight what we were hearing, including making calls to the government to say we are hearing what you are saying and it is not acceptable. But we also gave that message to leaders around the region.

I think they heard it, and I think we were able to actually stave off this turning into that kind of ethnic violence. There was clearly an effort to make a call to people to respond in that way. I think the Burundian people resisted, and we have to hope that they continue to resist. We have to continue to give them the wherewithal to resist these calls.

So there are some signs. It has not gotten to the point yet where we can call it a solid line drawn ethnic conflict, because, once that happens, I think it will be hard to turn it back.

Senator FLAKE. Thank you. With that and the appreciation of the committee, thank you for being here, and we will make time for the second panel.

Thank you, Assistant Secretary Thomas-Greenfield, for being here and for all your hard work. Thank you for always keeping us informed and working with us on this. We appreciate it.

Ms. THOMAS-GREENFIELD. Thank you very much.

Senator FLAKE. We will have a 2-minute break while the second panel takes its place. Thank you. [Break.]

Senator FLAKE. I appreciate the second panel being in place. Senator Markey will be back momentarily, so we will go ahead and get started.

Dr. Joseph Siegle is director of research, Africa Center for Strategic Studies, where his work focuses on the ongoing and long-term security challenges for African nations. Thank you for being here.

Thierry Vircoulon is the project director for Central Africa at the International Crisis Group. He joins us today all the way from Nairobi. Thank you for being here.

Vingy Nimuraba is dean's assistant and director for violence prevention programs at the School of Conflict Analysis and Resolution at George Mason University. Thank you for being here.

We look forward to your testimony, and we will go with Dr. Siegle.

STATEMENT OF DR. JOSEPH SIEGLE, DIRECTOR OF RESEARCH, AFRICA CENTER FOR STRATEGIC STUDIES, NATIONAL DEFENSE UNIVERSITY, WASHINGTON, D.C.

Dr. SIEGLE. All right, good afternoon, Chairman Flake. Thank you for the opportunity to speak with you today about the crisis in Burundi.

While frequently characterized in ethnic terms, the crisis in Burundi today is actually political in nature. It is an outcome of a political leader and a small cadre of allies gaming to perpetuate their hold on power passed through constitutionally mandated term limits.

This has triggered a breakdown in Burundi's popular and heretofore effective process of building a multiethnic democratic transition since the conclusion of the country's 12-year civil war in 2005, in which an estimated 300,000 Burundians lost their lives.

While there are pathways to resolving this crisis, it is important that a resolution be found quickly before the human costs worsen and the situation deteriorates to a point where any such solution becomes much more difficult and costly.

Finding a solution in Burundi has broader implications for the region as well. Already the Burundi crisis has created a burden for its neighbors, with 223,000 refugees, mostly in Rwanda and Tanzania. This is exacting a prolonged economic and social burden for these countries.

Africa's Great Lakes region also has been host to some of the most prolonged, vicious, and complicated conflicts on the continent over the past 2 decades. Further escalation in Burundi could at any time precipitate military intervention by neighboring Rwanda where the memories of genocide remain fresh. This in turn may spark a military response from other neighbors worried about Rwanda's influence in the region, recalling previous conflicts in the Democratic Republic of Congo.

Likewise, there are reports that Rwandan Hutu rebel groups operating out of the DRC, notably the Interahamwe, have been coming into Burundi in support government-aligned militias there.

Similarly, the outcome of the term limits battle in Burundi has political implications for the rest of Africa. Since 2000, there have been a dozen African leaders who have tried to circumvent term limits that were instituted to limit the monopolization of power and foster a culture of democratic transition in Africa.

Half of those leaders were successful in extending their time in office. The other half, however, facing concerted domestic and international opposition, were not. In fact, the trend since 2010 has been to block such attempted circumventions.

The outcome in Burundi, therefore, will impact the norm on the continent, where 19 of the 54 African leaders have been in power for more than a decade.

Furthermore, the tactics used in Burundi in pursuing a third term, overriding the constitution, bullying opponents, and then holding rump elections, set a particularly destabilizing precedent in Africa, if it is allowed to stand.

Despite the serious challenges involved, the crisis in Burundi is amenable to resolution. It is not rooted in deep structural differences within Burundian society. Moreover, a framework resolution already exists in the Arusha Accords that have guided the country out of its civil war. These accords are a popular social contract among Burundi's ethnically diverse population. They have become nothing less than a part of the social fabric and national identity in Burundi as part of its vision for a multiethnic democratic society.

So any diplomatic efforts we pursue should make clear that the Arusha Accords are the starting point for this.

So working in collaboration with regional mediation efforts, the United States can reinforce the Arusha political framework in the following five ways.

First, support the creation of a multiparty transitional government in Burundi. For the purpose of a transitional government, model experiences of Burkina Faso, Guinea, and Mali, to chart a course back to the constitutional framework of a free, fair, participatory electoral process.

These institution mechanisms were in place earlier in the year, before the April announcement. Consequently, the objective of this transitional phase would be to reestablish this democratic trajectory.

Second would be to support the deployment of an international peacekeeping force. In order for a political resolution and to foster a stable transition to Burundian crisis, the United States should logistically and financially support an international peacekeeping force under the auspices of the African Union and the United Nations. Such a force would serve as a buffer between rival armed groups to minimize the risk of escalation, enhance civilian protection, as well as to serve as a deterrent to the provocations that could trigger mass atrocities.

Third would be to sanction spoilers. The White House decision to issue targeted sanctions for individuals most responsible for the political violence is an effective way to demonstrate to Burundi's political elites that there are personal costs for their actions. The European Union and African Union have also imposed sanctions on individuals and entities. But the U.S. should be prepared to expand the scope and breadth of these sanctions as a way of exerting greater pressure on Burundian political actors.

Fourth, all non-statutory forces should be disbanded and forensic accounting should be made to identify those responsible for funding them. Given the central and unaccountable role that militias, particularly the Imbonerakure, are playing in intimidating and inflicting violence on the civilian population in Burundi, the United States should support the disbanding of these groups as part of any peacekeeping mandate.

Fifth, the free and independent flow of information should be restored. A prerequisite of any genuine domestic dialogue in the participatory political process in Burundi is going to be the restoration of an independent media and protections of the freedom of expression. The U.S. should call for the restoration of independent media outlets that have been closed by the Burundian Government. Until that time, the United States should expand funding to the

Voice of America, as well as networks of exiled from Burundian journalists across the region who can help report on events inside of Burundi.

The Government of Burundi should be called upon to immediately release all journalists who have been arrested. And in the absence of any domestic means to investigate the harassment and violence against journalists, the United States should also sponsor independent fact-finding missions by the African Union and the United Nations regarding the circumstances and parties responsible for journalists who have been killed or imprisoned in the course of trying to do their job of informing the public.

So in conclusion, the crisis in Burundi today is political. It is manufactured by a relatively small number of individuals who do not want to play by the democratic rulebook to which they came to power. In the process, they are attempting to undermine the multiethnic political framework that has been taking hold in Burundi.

Active international engagement at this point is going to be critical to restoring the Arusha Accords before the cycle of violence and fragmentation accelerates to a point that a solution becomes much more difficult and costly to Burundi, the region, and the international community.

Thank you very much.

[The prepared statement of Dr. Siegle follows:]

PREPARED STATEMENT OF DR. JOSEPH SIEGLE[1]

Chairman Flake, Ranking Member Markey, and fellow members of the Senate Subcommittee on Africa and Global Health Policy, thank you for the opportunity to speak with you today about the crisis in Burundi.

While frequently characterized in ethnic overtones pitting the majority Hutu population against the minority Tutsi, the crisis in Burundi today is not an ethnic conflict. This is a political crisis—an outcome of a political leader and a small cadre of allies aiming to perpetuate their hold on power past constitutionally-mandated term limits. This has triggered a breakdown in Burundi's popular and heretofore effective process of building a multi-ethnic democratic transition since the conclusion of the country's 12-year civil war in 2005 in which an estimated 300,000 Burundians lost their lives.

While there are pathways to resolving this crisis, it is important that a resolution be found quickly, before the situation deteriorates to a point of fragmentation and self-perpetuating ethnic conflict such that any solution becomes much more difficult and costly.

The current security situation

The crisis in Burundi was triggered on April 25, when incumbent President Pierre Nkurunziza announced he would seek a third term in office, despite a two-term limit in the country's constitution. Popular, peaceful protests organized by a multi-ethnic coalition of civil society organizations ensued. So too did an orchestrated campaign of intimidation by a youth militia, the Imbonerakure, which was established, trained, and armed by the ruling CNDD-FDD party for at least a year in advance. The repression escalated following an attempted military coup in May. Opposition strongholds, civil society representatives, and media were especially targeted.

This has led to the deaths of an estimated 500 people and the displacement of 280,000-350,000. Underscoring the political origins of this crisis-and the repercussions for dissent—many senior government officials from the CNDD-FDD opposed to Nkurunziza's bid for a third term have also fled to exile.

In the face of this intimidation and exodus, peaceful protests have waned and violent reprisals have emerged. In early August, a well-coordinated rocket attack killed

[1] Director of Research, Africa Center for Strategic Studies. All views expressed are those of the author and do not reflect an institutional position of the Africa Center for Strategic Studies or the Department of Defense.

the most feared military figure in the country, General Adolphe Nshimirimana. Reflecting an apparent decapitation strategy, several other senior military figures have also been assassinated or targeted. Several dozen police officers have also been attacked. In apparent retaliation, civil society and opposition political leaders or their family members have been killed.

Despite calls from African and international leaders to delay elections until the term limit controversy could be resolved through regional mediation efforts and stability restored, the CNDD-FDD held parliamentary and presidential elections in July. The elections were boycotted by opposition parties and were deemed to lack credibility by the United States, the African Union, the East African Community, the European Union, and the United Nations.

Keeping track of these fluid developments has been all the more difficult because Burundi's independent media outlets have been shuttered by government forces since May. Access to independent and corroborated sources of information has become more difficult.

The fear of genocide

Raising the stakes further, in an effort to mobilize support among the Hutu majority, the CNDD-FDD has been increasingly employing ethnically polarizing tactics. Purges among senior military and government officials have largely been ethnically based. In November, CNDD-FDD leaders began invoking ethnically incendiary language, recalling the pattern employed in the Rwandan genocide. Emblematic of this was a speech Burundian Senate President Reverien Ndikuriyo gave to supporters in Kirundi on November 3: "on this underlying issue, you have to pulverize, you have to exterminate—these people are only good for dying. I give you this order, go!" Similar statements were made by other senior government leaders including Pierre Nkurunziza. These remarks triggered a new surge of refugees toward Burundi's borders.

Swift international condemnation of such language, notably by President Obama, United States Ambassador to the United Nations Samantha Power, and an open letter by International Criminal Court (ICC) Prosecutor Fatou Bensouda that any invocation to ethnic violence would be used as evidence in a future ICC investigation, have led to the tempering of such inflammatory remarks. Nonetheless, the intimidation and targeted killings continue.

In short, the foundation for genocide—the mindset, climate of fear, and polarization—has been laid. Some Burundians have said the level of apprehension is now worse than during the civil war. Then, most of the killing was between armed combatants. Now civilians are also being targeted, causing a greater sense of vulnerability.

Various mediation efforts have been underway since April, led primarily by the African Union and the United Nations. These have been unsuccessful in dissuading Nkurunziza from his determination to hold onto power at all costs, however.

Nkurunziza's determined resistance to diplomacy and reason, even at risk of precipitating a new civil war and overturning all of the progress Burundi had made over the past decade, has led many Burundians to conclude that the only pressure he will respond to is military force.

Regional implications

Finding a resolution in Burundi has broader implications than for the country itself. Already the Burundi crisis has placed a burden on its neighbors with 240,000 refugees-mostly in Rwanda and Tanzania. During the 1993-2005 civil war there were 870,000 Burundian refugees, exacting a prolonged economic burden on the region.

Africa's Great Lakes region has also been host to some of the most prolonged, vicious, and complicated conflicts on the continent over the past two decades-from which the region has only recently been moving past. Further escalation against the population in Burundi could at any time precipitate a military intervention by neighboring Rwanda, where the memories of genocide remain fresh. This, in turn, may spark a military response from other neighbors worried about Rwanda's influence in the region and recalling previous conflicts in the Democratic Republic of the Congo (DRC). Likewise, there have already been reports of Rwandan Hutu rebel groups operating out of the DRC, notably the Interahamwe, coming into Burundi in support of government-aligned militias.

The outcome of the term limits battle in Burundi also has political implications for the rest of Africa. Since 2000, a dozen African leaders have tried to circumvent term limits that were instituted to limit the monopolization of power and foster a culture of democratic transitions in Africa. Half of those leaders were successful in extending their time in office. The other half, facing concerted domestic and international opposition, were not. In fact, the trend since 2010 has been to block such attempted circumventions. The outcome in Burundi, therefore, will shape the norm on the continent where 19 of 54 African leaders have been in power for more than a decade (and four for more than 30 years). Furthermore, the tactics used in pursuing a third term in Burundi—overriding the constitution, bullying opponents, and then holding rump elections—are a particularly dangerous precedent for Africa if allowed to stand.

Underlying factors to the Burundi crisis

Given the devastating social and economic costs to Burundi caused by Pierre Nkurunziza's decision to pursue a third term in office, as well as strong opposition from within his own party, it is reasonable to reflect on what some of the underlying motivations for this course of action may be.

In addition to the natural desire of many leaders in positions of authority to extend their time in power, Nkurunziza's efforts to retain control of the presidency likely stem from a Burundian political economy that rewards senior officials financially. Access to political power in Burundi allows for considerable control over public procurement processes, the mining sector, international financial assistance, and reimbursements for peacekeeping deployments. Moreover, presidential power affords control over state-owned monopolies, land and property sales, privatization procedures, as well as import and export restrictions. Burundi scores 159th out of 175 countries on Transparency International's ranking of most corrupt countries in the world. Furthermore, the government has forcibly intervened when its own anticorruption watchdog has inquired too deeply or publicly.

Another motivation for attempting to stay in power is the desire by some Hutu hardliners in the CNDD-FDD to break out of the Arusha Peace and Reconciliation Agreement for Burundi (referred to as the Arusha Accords). Their position is that the Accords are overly restrictive to Hutus, who comprise a strong majority in Burundi. The avoidance of term limits is a violation a key feature of the Accords. If this is accepted, it then offers prospects to renegotiate the entire political framework in Burundi in a manner that will be more conducive to hardline Hutu interests.

A framework for stability

Despite the serious challenges involved, this is a political crisis and is amenable to resolution. It is not rooted in deep structural differences within Burundian society. Moreover, a framework for resolution already exists in the Arusha Accords that has guided the country out of its civil conflict since 2000. This includes the precedent of political transitions. Burundi has experienced two peaceful transitions in power under the Accords, first in 2003 and again in 2005. Indeed, one of the greatest tragedies of the current crisis is the obscuring of the exemplary progress within Burundian society that has been made over the past 15 years. By stipulating that political power would not be dominated by either Hutus or Tutsis, the Arusha Accords promoted inter-ethnic political coalition building. This was true for nearly all of the major Burundian political parties including the CNDD-FDD.

Similar patterns took hold within civil society with the result being the fostering of an inter-ethnic national identity-a dramatic departure from the polarization of the past. Revealingly, the protests against Nkurunziza's bid for a third term were organized by these inter-ethnic civil society alliances involving more than 200 non-governmental organizations who were mutually motivated to upholding Burundi's fledgling democratic processes.

Perhaps the greatest headway was made within Burundi's military. Historically Tutsi-dominated, the military embarked on a comprehensive reform program in the mid-2000s that embodied the multi-ethnic principles of the Accords. Trust-building exercises were held at all levels of the military, Hutu and Tutsi recruits were trained together, and values of apolitical military professionalism were inculcated. While incomplete, the process demonstrated dramatic changes in attitudes about ethnicity within the military. Burundian troops also came to play a significant role in peacekeeping missions, especially through their contributions to the African Union's Mission in Somalia (AMISOM). Its five rotating battalions equate to more than 5,000 troops stationed in Somalia throughout the year. The result has been a relatively strong level of pride and military professionalism.

This professionalism has been on display during the political crisis. Despite extraordinary political pressures, the Burundian military has largely stayed neutral during the crisis. During the protests, soldiers regularly acted as a buffer between protesters and police and government-affiliated militias. Nkurunziza's inability to depend on the military for domestic political ends has constrained his behavior. That said, the ongoing efforts to politicize the military by arresting and purging Tutsi or moderate Hutu troops have placed great strains on this institution. Defections have ensued with as many as 300 military members having absconded with their weapons as a result.

The enormous value of Burundi's security sector reforms is underscored by how poorly the police, gendarmerie, and intelligence services have behaved in comparison to the military. These groups are made up mostly of former combatants from Burundi's civil war who were ineligible for integration into the military. Burundi's police and intelligence services, therefore, have remained politicized and are collaborating with the CNDD-FDD's youth league, the Imbonerakure, in cracking down on opposition and spearheading the pro-government violence.

The extent to which the Arusha Accords have become a part of the political fabric in Burundi is evidenced by the serious rift within the CNDD-FDD caused by Nkurunziza's pursuit of a third term and mobilization of support on an ethnic basis. Some 130 senior CNDD-FDD officials signed a petition in April requesting Nkurunziza to respect the Constitution and the Arusha Peace and Reconciliation Agreement. When this was rejected, over 140 CNDD-FDD members, including two senior vice-presidents, left the party (for safety concerns sometimes departing the country clandestinely before voicing their opposition). In July a coalition of opposition parties, senior defectors from the ruling party, and civil society leaders met in Addis Ababa, Ethiopia to form the National Council for the Restoration of the Arusha Accords (CNARED). It is leading a broad-based effort to engage in externally facilitated negotiations to establish an Inter-Burundian National Dialogue.

Role for external actors

Given the high levels of distrust among political parties and limited space for free expression, resolving the conflict in Burundi will require engagement by external actors. Diplomatic efforts in the region should continue to be the focal point for mediation efforts. The United States can support and enhance these initiatives in several ways.

• Support creation of a multi-party transitional government in Burundi

As part of its commitment to a political settlement in Burundi, the United States should support the creation of a transitional government in Burundi whose purpose is to oversee a political course back to a constitutional framework and a free, fair, and participatory electoral process. As the institutional mechanisms for a political transition were already in place earlier this year, the objective of this transitional phase would be to reestablish a path for this democratic trajectory. This transitional government of technocrats should be comprised of all leading political parties as well as representatives of civil society. Members of the transitional government would be barred from competing for political office in the succeeding elections. Having fulfilled his constitutionally mandated second term, Pierre Nkurunziza would not be eligible to participate in this transitional government or the subsequent presidential elections.

• All parties in Burundi must renew their commitment to the Arusha Peace and Reconciliation Agreement

Diplomatic efforts should make clear that the starting point for any political arrangement must be founded on the Arusha Accords. The Accords represent a social contract among Burundi's ethnically diverse population to end 12 years of civil war and, at times, genocidal massacres that dated back to Burundi's independence in 1960. The Arusha Accords were intended specifically to prevent future ethnic conflict and its provisions were included in Burundi's constitution. The highly popular Accords have become no less than a part of the fabric of Burundian national identity and its vision of a multiethnic, democratic society.

Under the Accords no single ethnic group can constitute more than half of the defense and security forces. Similarly, no ethnic group can hold more than two-thirds of local, county, and municipal positions. Across cabinet ministries, the diplomatic service, and the institutions supporting democracy such as the National Electoral Commission, Constitutional Court, National Assembly, and National Commission on Human Rights, no party in power can enjoy more than 60 percent representation.

• Support deployment of international peacekeeping forceIn order to support a political resolution and foster a stable transition to the Burundi crisis, the United States should logistically and financially support an international peacekeeping force (likely comprising 3,000-5,000 troops) under the auspices of the African Union and/or United Nations. As at the end of the civil war, such a force would serve as a buffer between rival armed groups to minimize the risk of escalation, enhance civilian protection, as well as to serve as a deterrent to provocations that could trigger mass atrocities. Deploying a peacekeeping force would also serve as a confidence-building measure for all sides, which would help provide assurances to those in exile and among all parties to the conflict that their return and participation in the political dialogue will be supported by institutional safeguards. The African Union has previously called on its members to be prepared to support such a mission. U.N. Security Council Resolution 2248, furthermore, reminds all of the ICC's jurisdiction and welcomes the deployment of African Union monitors and military experts.

- Sanction spoilers

The White House's decision to issue targeted sanctions on four individuals most responsible for the political violence-from both the government and opposition-is an effective way of demonstrating to Burundi's political elites the personal costs of their actions. The European Union and African Union have also imposed sanctions on a list of individuals and entities.

The United States has also suspended Burundi from eligibility for the preferential trade benefits that come from the African Growth and Opportunity Act (AGOA). The EU is debating whether to suspend Burundi's trade privileges. Belgium and other European bilateral donors have suspended aid to a number of development projects and stopped cooperation with the Burundian police. This is particularly significant since aid accounts for 54 percent of Burundian government expenditures.

The United States should be prepared to expand the scope and breadth of these targeted sanctions as a means of exerting greater pressure on Burundi's political actors to restore the Arusha Accords and demonstrate a sustained United States commitment to a political resolution. With this aim in mind, the United States should offer its cooperation in evidence- gathering to any International Criminal Court investigation that is undertaken.

- All non-statutory forces must be disbanded and forensic accounting should identify those responsible for funding them.

Given the central (and unaccountable) role that militias, particularly the Imbonerakure, are playing in intimidating and inflicting violence on the civilian population in the Burundi conflict, the United States should support the disbanding of these groups as part of any peacekeeping mandate. The United States should also make available any information, including the forensic accounting of financial flows to these groups so as to hold responsible those political actors who are sponsoring these militias.

- The free and independent flow of information should be restored

A prerequisite to a genuine domestic dialogue and a participatory political process in Burundi is the restoration of independent media and protections for freedom of expression. Independent reporting and access to information are also essential ingredients to maintaining domestic and international accountability. The United States should call for the restoration of all independent print, broadcast, and digital media outlets that have been closed by the Burundian government. Until that time, the United States should expand funding to the Voice of America and exiled Burundian journalists who can tap their networks to report on events inside of Burundi.

The Government of Burundi should be called on to immediately release all journalists who have been arrested. In the absence of any domestic mechanisms to investigate the harassment and violence against journalists, the United States should also sponsor an independent fact-finding mission by the African Union and United Nations regarding the circumstances and parties responsible for journalists who have been killed or imprisoned in the course of trying to do their jobs of informing the general public.

Conclusion

The crisis in Burundi today is political-manufactured by a relatively small number of individuals who do not want to play by the democratic rulebook through which they came to power. In the process, they are attempting to undermine the multi-ethnic political framework that has provided Burundi a pathway away from cycles of genocide to peace and stability. Active international engagement at this point is critical to restoring the Arusha Accords before the cycle of violence and fragmentation accelerates and finding a political solution becomes much more difficult and costly to Burundi, the region, and the international community.

Senator FLAKE. Thank you.
Mr. Vircoulon?

STATEMENT OF THIERRY VIRCOULON, CENTRAL AFRICA PROJECT DIRECTOR, INTERNATIONAL CRISIS GROUP, NAIROBI, KENYA

Mr. VIRCOULON. Thank you, Chairman. I appreciate the opportunity to appear this afternoon on behalf of the International Crisis Group before the Senate Foreign Relations Committee to discuss the current political and security crisis in Burundi. We want to thank the chairman and members of the committee for calling U.S. attention to an already severe humanitarian crisis and one that has a potential for mass atrocities and regional destabilization.

The Crisis Group has been following developments in Burundi for almost 2 decades, and we have warned repeatedly about these crises building under President Pierre Nkurunziza, one with political origins, as it was said, but with clear ethnic undercurrents.

The first phase of the present crisis began with the 2010 election. Those polls were a logistical success but a political failure, leaving political institutions dominated by the ruling party. Immediately following those elections, the government launched a post-electoral campaign of extrajudicial killings and forced its main opponents out of the country.

As a result, civil society and independent media became the only dissenting voices. From 2010 to 2014, there was a steady polarization, socioeconomic discontent, and further closing of political space.

The second phase of the crisis started in 2014 and centered on the growing evidence that President Nkurunziza intended to run for a third term, violating the Arusha agreement.

The third phase of the crisis started in April this year with street protests against President Nkurunziza's candidacy for a third term.

The present phase of the crisis—armed confrontation—corresponded with President Nkurunziza securing a third-term mandate in July after an election that the African Union and the European Union decided not to observe because of political and security conditions in the country.

Even beyond the humanitarian tragedy unfolding in Burundi, the regime now looks more and more like a failed police state. Regional spillover no longer is just a threat, as has been said, but a reality.

The present patterns of violence are a reminder of what happened before the civil war broke out in 1993. For the Burundians, the story is repeating itself. This deja vu feeling and the memories of the civil war are the reasons why more than 200,000 Burundians have fled their country since the start of this year.

One of the fundamental reasons why this crisis matters for Burundi, Africa, and the international community is that it challenges the Arusha peace agreement that was painstakingly negotiated during 4 years to bring peace to a country where 300,000 had died.

One of the most glaring failures of Arusha sponsors was not enforcing respect for the results of international mediation. Mediation brokered a deal for the return of the opponents in exile in 2013 with the view of making the 2015 elections inclusive.

Special envoys from the U.S., the EU, Belgium, France, the U.K. and other countries also enabled a dialogue led by the U.N. special envoy between the opposition and the government to try and bring peace during the street protests earlier this year. However, the aim of an inclusive electoral process was gutted by President Nkurunziza's insistence on running again.

The mediation was officially handed over to the Ugandan President Yoweri Museveni, but there has been no progress. The resumption of an externally mediated dialogue is now the only option.

The decision of the U.S. Government to support an international dialogue is, at this stage, very important. U.S. President Barack Obama's 27 October decision to exclude Burundi from the African Growth and Opportunity Act is an important signal, but it is not enough.

The African Union Peace and Security Council has been most outspoken in demanding an end to violence, a resumption of a facilitated dialogue, and threatening the use of an African Union intervention force. But the African Union members do not want to bypass President Museveni and the East African Community.

Right now, the Westerners are waiting for the African Union. The African Union is waiting for President Museveni. And the people of Burundi are waiting for the end of violence.

If there is no externally mediated dialogue, the likely scenarios include a new coup, the emergence of a guerilla force in the countryside, and/or a large-scale repression against the rebellious districts of Bujumbura.

Therefore, the resumption of a dialogue between the opposition and the government is absolutely essential. This implies the formation of an international mediation team supported by the U.S. and the European Union with additional sanctions against those responsible for violence.

The agenda of the internationally mediated dialogue should be open, but it should include the Arusha agreement.

If there is a need to halt atrocity, and if an African Union-led peace implementation mission cannot be deployed quickly, the U.N. should be planning to bring MONUSCO's Force Intervention Brigade into action.

In addition, the African Union should be examining how it could replace Burundian troops in AMISOM, if that becomes necessary.

It also must be stressed to Rwanda and Tanzania that they must play a constructive role in the present crisis.

The wait-and-see attitude of the international community during the past 4 years is part of the reason why the crisis has brought us to this point. There is now urgency for more coherent and determined international action to halt the country's further disintegration and prevent more violence within and beyond Burundi's border.

Thank you for your attention.

[The statement of Mr. Vircoulon follows:]

PREPARED STATEMENT OF THIERRY VIRCOULON

I appreciate the opportunity to appear this afternoon on behalf of the International Crisis Group before the Senate Foreign Relations Africa Subcommittee to discuss the current political and security crisis in Burundi. We want to thank the chairman and members of the Committee for calling U.S. attention to an already severe humanitarian crisis and one that has the potential for mass atrocities and regional destabilization.

The International Crisis Group came into being because our founders believed that too often, major powers and international organizations ignored the cables, however incomplete they might be, coming from Rwanda, or Srebrenica or the Congo. After the Cold War, there seemingly no longer were strategic linkages from those countries affecting major powers, other than the sheer horror of the human suffering being inflicted.

We are an independent, non-partisan, non-governmental organization that provides field-based analysis, policy advice and recommendations to governments, the United Nations, the European Union and other multilateral organizations on the prevention and resolution of deadly conflict. We were founded in 1995 by distinguished diplomats, statesmen and opinion leaders. Our president is Jean-Marie Guehenno, former head of U.N. peacekeeping, and our board of national and international leaders includes four former heads of state and eight former foreign or defense ministers and distinguished African leaders including Cheryl Carolus, former South African High Commissioner to the UK and Secretary General of the African National Congress; Mo Ibrahim, president of Ibrahim Foundation; and Ayo Obe, Nigerian lawyer and human rights activist. U.S. foreign policy leaders on our board include Ambassador and former Undersecretary of Political Affairs Thomas Pickering, former NATO Supreme Commander Wesley Clark, former Senator Olympia Snowe, former career Ambassador Mort Abramowitz and former Secretary of the Treasury Lawrence Summers.

Crisis Group has been following developments in Burundi for almost two decades, and we have warned repeatedly about this crisis building under President Pierre Nkurunziza, one with political origins but with clear ethnic undercurrents. The first phase of the present crisis began with the 2010 elections. Those polls were a logistical success but political failure. The opposition only participated in the communal elections and boycotted the national ones, charging the government with unfairly tilting the playing field, but thereby leaving national political institutions dominated by the National Council for the Defense of Democracy-Forces for the Defense of Democracy (CNDD-FDD).

Immediately following those elections, the government launched a repressive postelectoral campaign of extrajudicial killings and forced its main opponents out of the country. As a result, civil society and independent media became the only dissenting voices. From 2010 to 2014, there was steady polarization, socio-economic discontent and further closing of political space. It included a failed constitutional review, public disputes between civil society watchdogs and the government, and the government arming the youth wing of the CNDD-FDD known as the Imbonerakure to maintain a tight grip on the countryside. The Nkurunziza administration established a near monopoly and corrupt control over state resources, bribed and coerced opposition party leaders and over time used national police and security forces to enforce authoritarian governance.

The earlier political deterioration exploded finally into the second phase of the crisis in 2014 centered on the growing evidence that Nkurunziza intended to run for a third term-violating the Arusha Accord which had ended the country's 12 year civil war. During the electoral preparations, the government and the opposition disagreed on almost everything, from the composition of the local electoral commissions to the registration of voters, stripping its legitimacy from the start. At the end of 2014, all the unsolved problems of the previous four years had resurfaced. With the ruling party rejecting any consensual approach, opposition and civil society had no faith in the electoral process as a means to achieve political change.

The third phase of the crisis started in April this year with street protests against President Nkurunziza's candidacy for a third term. After the president managed to obtain the blessing of the constitutional court and to silence those who opposed his candidacy within his own party, demonstrations in Bujumbura, the capital city, quickly turned violent. Daily confrontations occurred between the security forces/Imbonerakure and a coalition of political opposition/civil society organizations who enjoyed the moral support of the Catholic Church. Two key developments happened during this phase. First, the army, which had initially played a positive role by interposing its forces between demonstrators and police to halt conflict, became increasingly fractured leading finally to high-ranking officers organizing a failed coup in May. Second, given increasing rifts within the CNDD-FDD and fearing for their lives, many moderate leaders of the ruling party fled the country, leaving the radicals in complete control of the party and the state. Regional and international attempts to mediate the crisis in June and July only managed to delay elections without substantially improving the conditions under which they were held.

The final phase of the crisis-armed confrontation-corresponded with President Nukurnziza securing a third-term mandate in July after fraught elections declared unfair by virtually every observer, including the African Union, the European

Union, the U.S. and other governments. Nightly police raids and execution-style operations followed in districts of Bujumbura where many regime opponents lived and have led now to the militarization of the political conflict, with dead bodies dumped in the streets each night and grenade attacks occurring almost daily. A normal day in Bujumbura starts with the counting of the night's death toll.

Why the Burundi crisis matters

Even beyond the the humanitarian tragedy unfolding in Burundi, the regime now looks more and more like a failed police state. There is violent and open confrontation between armed government forces and a large opposition consortium, also increasingly armed. President Nkurunziza and the leaders of the ruling party are bunkering themselves; the economy is barely functioning (according to the IMF, GDP will have shrunk by 7.2 per cent this year); many businessmen and women, civil society leaders and journalists are out of the country;security institutions are politicized and divided. The stability of Burundi is in jeopardy with dangerous regional consequences.

Regional spillover no longer is just a threat, but a reality. Population flight already has produced a refugee crisis with several hundred thousand Burundians fleeing across the country's borders in eight months. The formal refugee numbers, undoubtedly understated, of 215,000 include 70,000 in Rwanda, more than 100,000in western Tanzania and the rest in DRC and Uganda. Serious tensions with Rwanda include the severing of diplomatic ties and Kigali accusing Burundi of tolerating the presence of Rwandan Hutu FDLR (Democratic Forces for the Liberation of Rwanda, an armed militia that may still include former genocidaires) and Bujumbura accusing Kigali of recruiting, training and arming Burundian refugees in refugee camps in Rwanda.

The pattern of violence changed immediately following the reelection of president Nkurunziza. Targeted assassinations of key personalities in both camps have taken place (General Nishirimana, Colonel Bikomagu, an assassination attempt of Pierre Claver Mbonimpa, a well-known human rights activist, and the recent murder of one of his sons; and another attack on the army chief of staff) along with mortar attacks against the presidential palace. Both sides are radicalizing. Government officials are reviving the rhetoric from the civil war of 1993-2005. The president made public an ultimatum giving the "criminals" seven days to lay down arms. Reverien Ndikuriyo, the Senate president, cryptically warned on 1 November that the police would soon go to "work" and asked district heads to identify "elements which are not in order". The language is unambiguous to Burundians and chillingly similar to that used in Rwanda in the 1990s before the genocide. The opposition is organizing in exile and a platform was created in Addis Ababa by politicians (including the moderates from the ruling party), civil society leaders and former military officers. The present patterns of violence are a reminder of what happened before the civil war broke out in 1993. For the Burundians, the story is repeating itself. This deja vu feeling and the memories of the civil war are the reasons why so many of them have left their country.One of the fundamental reasons why this crisis matters for Burundi, Africa and the international communities is that it challenges the Arusha peace agreement of August 2000 that was painstakingly negotiated during four years to bring peace to a country where 300,000 had died in more than a decade of conflict. That accord, negotiated with the facilitation of two African presidents (President Julius Nyerere and President Nelson Mandela) and endorsed by the U.N., AU, US France and the EU, institutionalized political and ethnic power-sharing between Hutu and Tutsi. The Arusha agreement explicitly mentions the two-term limit for presidents (article 7). While there had been a long list of violations of the Arusha agreement since its signing and a failure in the constitutional review attempt of 2014, it was the violation of the no third term provision that was the straw that finally broke the camel's back.

In its report Bye Bye Arusha, written in 2012, Crisis Group warned that the ruling party was distancing itself from the Arusha agreement and listed all the violations of the peace accord. The CNDD-FDD never genuinely adhered to its principles and blocked the implementation of those which were detrimental to its monopoly of power. For instance, it discarded the creation of a special tribunal to deal with the crimes of the civil war and opted only for the creation of a truth and reconciliation commission whose work has not even started. Indeed the issue of post-conflict justice has remained the elephant in the room during the two mandates of president Nkurunziza who has been granted provisional amnesty. The present crisis also has demonstrated another critical violation of the Arusha agreement: the politicization of the security forces. The ruling party gradually distanced itself from the Arusha agreement because most Arusha guarantors did not follow up on their commitments to long-term political engagement and resorted to a near completely private diplomatic approach without firm consequences until very recently, despite clear signs of authoritarian actions and violation of the Arusha accord.

One of the most glaring failures by Arusha sponsors was not enforcing respect for the results of international mediation. Mediation brokered a deal for the return of the opponents in exile in 2013 with the view of making the 2015 elections inclusive. Special envoys from the U.S., the EU, Belgium, France, the UK and other countries also enabled a dialogue led by the U.N. special envoy between the opposition coalition and the government to try and bring peace during street protests earlier this year. However, the aim of an inclusive electoral process was gutted by Nkurunziza's insistence on running for a third term. The mediation was officially handed over to the Ugandan president Yoweri Museveni this past summer but, despite informal consultations, no meeting has happened yet under his chairmanship. The resumption of the dialogue is the only option at this stage but only informal consultations have been held and the most that is hoped is that a meeting may happen before the end of the year.

As Burundi's civil war was ended by an agreement negotiated by African leaders, Western governments have again waited for an African solution, i.e. a regionally mediated dialogue. Unfortunately, times have changed. South Africa has disengaged from Burundi and its present government seems disinterested in preserving Mandela's legacy. The East African Community (EAC) has been mandated to find a solution but is too divided. In addition, its chief mediator, Ugandan President Museveni, in power since 1986, is himself busy with the preparation of elections in early 2016.

U.S. President Barack Obama's 27 October decision to exclude Burundi from the "African Growth and Opportunity Act" is an important signal of the U.S.'s growing concern, but it is not enough. The African Union (AU) Peace and Security Council (PSC) has been most outspoken in demanding an end to violence and a resumption of a facilitated dialogue, issuing a strong communique and threatening the use of an African Union intervention force, but does not want to bypass president Museveni and the EAC.Right now the westerners are waiting for the AU, the AU is waiting for president Museveni and the people of Burundi are waiting for the end of violence. If there is no regionally mediated dialogue, the likely scenarios include: a new coup attempt, the emergence of a guerila force in the countryside and/or a large scale repression against the rebellious districts of Bujumbura.Another reason why what happens in Burundi matters is it could set a dangerous precedent among its neighbors. While there are substantial differences in each of its neighbors where the third term issue also is a matter of dispute, the potential for political unraveling appears greatest in the DRC where a third term for its president Joseph Kabila constitutes a similar violation of the peace agreement and the DRC constitution.The way forwardThe resumption of the dialogue between the opposition and the government is absolutely essential. This implies the formation of an international mediation team with AU, EAC, International organization of the French speaking countries (IOF), U.N. representatives, supported by the U.S. and the EU with additional sanctions against those responsible for egregious violence, like those the U.S. announced last week--to put pressure on the reluctant stakeholders.The agenda of the internationally mediated dialogue should be open and it should include the Arusha agreement. As the stumbling block of the post-conflict regime, the Arusha agreement is the reference point in every political discussion about Burundi but a frank discussion is needed about the future of the Arusha agreement and its values that have underpinned the hard-won peace in Burundi. The Arusha agreement is at the core of the Burundi crisis and therefore it must not be taboo. Some 15 years after its signing it is legitimate to ask whether some changes—but only if adopted consensually—are needed.

The U.N. should be planning, if an AU led peace implementation mission cannot be deployed quickly to bring MONUSCO's FIB into action if there is a need to halt atrocities. In addition, the AU should be examining how it could replace Burundian troops in AMISOM if that becomes necessary. In addition, the AU, the U.S., UK and other concerned members of the international community should quietly stress to the Rwandan and new Tanzanian governments that they must play more constructive roles.

The wait-and-see attitude of the international community during the past four years is part of the reason why the crisis has brought us to this point. There is now urgency for more coherent and determined international action to halt the country's further disintegration and expanded violence within and beyond Burundi's borders.

Senator FLAKE. Thank you.
We now turn to Vigny Nimuraba.

STATEMENT OF SIXTE VIGNY NIMURABA, DEAN'S ASSISTANT AND DIRECTOR OF VIOLENCE PREVENTION PROGRAM, THE SCHOOL FOR CONFLICT ANALYSIS AND RESOLUTION, GEORGE MASON UNIVERSITY, ARLINGTON, VIRGINIA

Mr. NIMURABA. Chairman Flake, Ranking Member Cardin, members of the subcommittee, thank you for the invitation to appear here today to discuss the political and security crisis in Burundi. I thank also the School for Conflict Analysis and Resolution at George Mason University.

I am Burundian, and I just returned. This testimony reflects the discussions I had with key stakeholders, as well as common Burundians, from all sides—different people, different understandings of the crisis, different approaches to resolution.

From the government perspective, a core pillar of Arusha Accords is ethnic quotas, and this remains unquestionable by both government and opposition in Burundi. Virtually everyone agrees that it is still a good thing to have security forces made up of 50 percent Hutu and 50 percent Tutsi troops. Although the population is actually divided into approximately 85 percent Hutu and 15 percent Tutsi citizens, the government holds to the principle of 40 percent Tutsi and 60 percent Hutu staffers at any administrative leadership posts in the country.

Burundi's leadership has called upon all organizations, national and international, to check and make sure they respect those ethnic quotas to reflect the makeup of the population.

One of the major achievements of the past 15 years is the power of unity over ethnic divisions. The Burundian people can distinguish ethnic groups from political and personal interests.

It is widely agreed that Burundian people need peace. People in the countryside do not care about presidential terms or nuances of constitutional law. While some people want economic support, such as chemical fertilizers or seeds, others want jobs and equal opportunities.

The capital city is the place where the political classes live. That may be the reason why there is violence now, and that has a lot to do with our own history.

Current government leaders see Western countries as denying the principles of democracy and sovereignty of Burundi. There is an underreported cold war competition between the two major powers, China and Russia on one side and the West on the other. Exploited mineral resources like nickel and uranium play a major role in that commercial conflict.

The concept of genocide is being invented to show that the situation is chaotic and, therefore, to call for external military intervention. It is, however, critical that atrocity prevention efforts take seriously the specific context in which violence is unfolding.

The current government is not opposed to dialogue. Inclusive dialogue has started among all Burundians. This dialogue will continue with members of the diaspora. However, the dialogue will not include people who were involved in the failed coup of May 2015.

In dealing with people involved in the protests, the first group made up of underage prisoners has been released and the Red Cross was in charge of bringing them back to their families. Yesterday, around 100 youth involved in the protests were released, and the African Union was present at that release.

People were released after completing a civic education program. This initiative will continue, and it needs to be supported.

Finally, the government has issued a strong request that all people involved in the process of addressing the current crisis to visit the whole country and see how different some suburbs of Bujumbura look in comparison to other areas, if they wish to write accurate reports on Burundi.

The opposition's major motivation to fight is unequal opportunities. There is some kind of collaboration between the youth who fighting with some current army forces. The only way peace can be restored is if opposition can be involved in the discussion and dialogue, which would be inclusive. That must take place in a safe zone.

Religious leaders, especially the Catholic Church, are calling both parties to dialogue without pushing too hard.

Civil society operates under fear. Civil society requests the government to stop the immediate act of harassment, intimidation, and arbitrary detention against members of civil society organizations, journalists, and other human right activists and peace-builders, as well as members of their families.

Burundian civil society would like to see the establishment of an independent and rigorous inquiry in order to establish responsibility for the violence observed in Burundi since April 2015.

There is a problem is the new education system—bachelor, master's, doctorate—which was launched with insufficient studies in terms of implementation and transition from the previous system.

Some week-long basic workshops were conducted to equip educators with skills to teach new courses, such as English, Swahili, music, and arts. Educators themselves testify, however, that they did not learn enough to allow them to teach those courses adequately.

The deteriorating education system is a real threat to security in Burundi. If young people do not have access to good education and consequently to good jobs, no matter how hard we work to address the current issue, violence will remain and will not cease.

Rwanda has an active role in the Burundi crisis. Hopefully, the international community will request Rwanda to stop such tactics. Other counties such as Tanzania, DRC, and Uganda have also a major role to play, they can really act and stop violence in Burundi.

Some of the recommendations include the need to improve the economy, job creation, investment, and opportunities for youth and other people who are able to work.

Second, we should improve education programs, both long-term and short-term, with regard to peace education.

Post-traumatic stress disorder is a continuing problem in Burundi. We need to create a substantial program of trauma healing that will be implemented nationwide. This would also include non-violence activities and teaching.

Some other suggestions: one, help the government disarm all militia, regardless of political affiliation; two, request the government to restore the freedom of expression, allowing private media to reopen; three, allow civil society to operate freely and to reopen the bank accounts that have been frozen for investigation purposes, and this goes along with training of civil society personnel and journalists to improve the capacity for reporting and acting responsibly; four, strengthen the African Union human rights observers and require them to have toll-free phones to allow every Burundian to reach them and to report misconduct; five, urge the Burundian Government to have conflict resolution experts working with the national commission for dialogue to focus on long-term goals and sustainability of peace in Burundi; six, urge the Rwandan Government not to continue its interference in the Burundian crisis and, if necessary, put in place some sanctions against Rwanda; seven, provide generous humanitarian support to all displaced and support an extensive campaign for refugees to return to Burundi once security is restored; finally, pressure and sanctions will not work but will radicalize parties to the conflict in Burundi. The U.S. and the international community should look for other ways, other collaborative ways, to address the current issue.

Thank you.

[The prepared statement of Mr. Nimuraba follows:]

PREPARED STATEMENT OF SIXTE VIGNY NIMURABA

Chairman Flake, Ranking Member Markey, members of the subcommittee:

Thank you for the invitation to appear here today to discuss the political and security crisis in Burundi.

By way of background, I currently serve as the Dean's Assistant and Director of Violence Prevention for the Genocide Prevention Program / GPP in the School for Conflict Analysis and Resolution (S-CAR) at George Mason University (GMU), where I am also pursuing a doctoral degree. I have had extensive experience working with Burundian civil society and non-governmental organizations to promote peace, conflict prevention, social cohesion, and integration of returnees in local communities.

During my four-year tenure with Ligue Iteka, the oldest and largest civil society organization in Burundi, I collaborated closely with UNHCR and other national and international human rights organizations to foster peaceful coexistence. In my capacity as regional coordinator within Ligue Iteka's Monitoring of Returnees Project, I first coordinated resettlement and social cohesion activities in five northern provinces (Ngozi, Kirundo, Kayanza, Muyinga and Karusi) and was then promoted to the position of southern regional coordinator, covering the provinces of Makamba, Bururi, and Rutana, which together had a significantly larger population of returnees and a remarkably larger number of land conflicts to mitigate.

Before joining Ligue Iteka, I held different positions in local and international organizations such as VISPE, Care International, and CNLS. This work inspired my passion to dedicate my life to the quest for peaceful coexistence and social cohesion in Burundi and the African Great Lakes region, which eventually brought me to this hearing room today.

Mr. Chairman, in your letter of invitation to present this testimony, you posed questions in three broad areas of interest. First, what have I learned during my recent trips to Burundi about the perspectives of average citizens toward the current political situation and prospects of violence that may disrupt their lives? Second, what have I learned in discussions with members of the government and opposition parties about how Burundi can prevent further political violence and move toward a clearer path of reconciliation? And third, how do I perceive the role of Burundi's neighbors in the region to facilitate the peace process, diffuse tensions, and get the country "back on track"—plus what role can the United States and other international partners play in improving the situation?

I would like to address each of these issues separately, although you may see some overlap in the discussion. While these are preliminary thoughts, I will be happy to answer your questions and provide clarification or additional information today or in writing later to supplement the hearing record.

A core pillar of Arusha Accords is "ethnic quotas" and this remain unquestionable by both government and opposition in Burundi. Virtually everyone agrees that it is still a good thing to have security forces made up of 50 percent Hutu and 50 percent

Tutsi troops. Although the population is actually divided into approximately 85 percent Hutu and 14 percent Tutsi citizens, the government holds to the principle of 40 percent Tutsi and 60 percent Hutu staffers at any administrative leadership post in the country, from the presidency to the administration of the smallest entity, which is the "hill" (administration collinaire). Burundi's leadership has called upon all organizations, national and international, to check and make sure they respect those ethnic quotas, to reflect the make-up of the country's population.

One of the major achievements of the past fifteen years is the power of unity over ethnic divisions. The Burundian people can distinguish ethnic groups from political and personal interests. After decades of artificial segregation, the Arusha Accords and subsequent constitutional and legal reforms successfully brought Hutu and Tutsi together to work in the same office, to plan and implement projects jointly, to govern and to be governed together. At the end of the day, the Burundian people discovered that any leader can be good or bad regardless whether he is Hutu or Tutsi. Now the majority of Hutu and Tutsi know that they have the same destiny and therefore must struggle together and celebrate what they have together. This shared struggle that both Hutu and Tutsi now experience is, however, endangered by a small number of older people who retain vivid memories of ethnic hate the violence it spewed. These few sadly try to embed their fears among younger generations. Our hope is that newer generations—today's young people and their children and grandchildren—will remain united and refuse to inherit the dangerous ideology of the past.

It is widely agreed that the Burundian people need peace. Yet, as in most countries, many people among the government and among the opposition claim that the majority of the populace supports their own cause. Yet the reality is that both Hutu and Tutsi have bad memory of the civil war. They still remember human and material losses caused by that war and they would not like to see this happen again. People in the countryside do not care about president terms or the nuances of constitutional law. They likely know nothing about what the Arusha Accords say about the president's term limits; what they remember is that there has been a popular president who does community service with them and who plays soccer with them.

The people's desire for peace is reflected in how many armed people have been caught and denounced by other citizens, as was the case in Muyinga, Kayanza, Cibitoke, Bujumbura, and elsewhere. The Burundian people do not want any fellow citizens to be left behind because he may endanger the sustainability of peace that they reached the hard way. What they say when you ask them is, "Can you please tell our leaders to ask what the opposition needs and share some of the parliamentary seats with them? They should give them something of political value so that politicians do not lead us into another civil war".

Another question that should be raised is why the violence is mainly occurring only in few discrete areas, especially in some suburbs of Bujumbura, the capital city. One answer is that the capital city is the place where the political classes live. Since independence in 1963, the ruling class and their families have taken advantage of the opportunity to move to Bujumbura to seek an even better life than what they had in their home towns. It was the best place to live for people doing business, military families, and people searching for both government and private-sector jobs. This was also related to the how land distribution had been done in the past few decades, as well as property leasing requirements, rent-to-buy procedures, and so forth.

The Arusha Accords—The Burundian people's engagement for unity and forgiveness

Although the 2005 Arusha Accords did contribute to peace in Burundi, most of the work was done by the people themselves. The Arusha Accords were a blessing from both the international community and leaders of the then-opposition and President Buyoya's administration. In effect, the Arusha Accord was more about power sharing than peace and reconciliation per se—although all those were components of the agreement.

What outside observers tend to forget is that the Burundian people, no matter what side they were on as the civil war approached its end, were exhausted. They were tired of war and daily killings and fighting that had been occurring for more than 12 years. People started to ask the fighters to engage in dialogue that could bring peace back, Hutus, on one side, were pressing rebels to stop violent means and start negotiations with the government; on the other side, Tutsi were also demanding the Tutsi-dominated army and government to find ways of talking with the rebels in order to stop the violence.

Even before and during the civil war, there were many communities that had already overcome ethnic divisions. Some Hutus had started to help Tutsis whose houses were destroyed to make bricks and help them return to their properties. The only Tutsis who remained in internally displaced person (IDP) camps were those who had direct ties with people involved in leadership position, those with business activities, and several others who were better off compared to the rest of Burundian population. Those wealthy families decided either to rent houses for their IDP families in cities and suburbs, because they had financial means to support them from there. Other Tutsi families returned or had already returned to their native towns and villages and were interacting productively with Hutu residents on a daily basis.

For Hutu communities, the majority of them had also left regroupment camps (camps de regroupements) which were established by the government in order to separate innocent people from those who were then called rebels.

Before the Arusha agreements, there were Hutu and Tutsi communities which had already started to share lives and to help each other, letting go the past ethnic conflict and the losses it caused. Burundians were thirsty for peace, unity and reconciliation.

Some major achievements must be acknowledged:

a. With the return of security, people do not spend nights in the bush or in holes fearing military attacks or rebel group attacks

b. Hutus and Tutsi live together; no matter what has been said, all ethnic groups remain united

c. Most of the Burundian people are less interested in politics, term limits, and leadership positions, but more on economic opportunity and their survival.

d. Little by little, people are realizing that very few leaders, if any, are more sincerely interested in the people's wellbeing and interests than they are in their personal goals, in most cases financial interests. There are no more leaders who love and care about their people.

Different people, different understanding of the crisis, different approaches to resolution

Current government leaders see few policy issues dividing government from the opposition. For them the problem is between the current government and Western countries that are denying the principles of democracy and sovereignty of Burundi.There is an underreported cold war competition between the major powers—China and Russia on one side and the West on the other. Unexploited mineral resources like nickel and uranium play a major role in that commercial conflict. Exploration for minerals is being performed by two Russian companies. The government, however, is now open to sharing extraction with any other countries, especially since it became clear that the minerals from Nyabikere and Waga are more numerous than it was previously believed. There is so much to extract that more than one company can be granted a concession.

According to current Burundian leaders, the country does not have only one option (a partnership with the United States and European Union). It has also another option to partner with Russia and China in different sectors. Even if it may require some time to decide how to construct such an alignment, it is not politically or commercially impossible.

The army was able to contain violence when some armed groups attacked from Cibitoke in December 2014 and, more recently, when a group of armed fighters came from Rwanda entering through Buyumpu and Kabarore. Note that around 200 fighters were arrested during the operation in Kibira, where those groups were heading.

The concept of genocide is being invented in minds of the opposition to show that the situation is chaotic and they therefore call for external military intervention. As Michael Broache of the University of Tampa and Kate Cronin-Furman of Stanford University noted in the Washington Post on November 15, Burundi's situation is "not, nor will it ever be, 'another Rwanda.' It's critical that atrocity prevention efforts take seriously the specific context in which violence is unfolding. Crying 'genocide' instead of calling it what it is—political violence, with the possibility of escalating into crimes against humanity—does nobody any favors, least of all the victims." In response to calls for military intervention, Patrick Hajayandi of the Institute for Justice and Reconciliaton wrote in the Daily Maverick on the same date that "Foreign military intervention could potentially cause a tense situation to become incendiary. A military intervention is likely to radicalize both parties, and pit them against each other, creating an all-out civil war."

Views of the government

The tension between Burundi and other countries as well as the international community started when some countries issued statements that scheduled elections could not take place because there were no required conditions for them to be "fair."

Despite the withdrawal of international support, the elections for parliament and president took place nearly on schedule and the government is ready to maintain that achievement through any means.

In contrast to what many people say, the current government is not opposed to dialogue. Inclusive dialogue has started among all Burundians and this dialogue will include members of the diaspora. The government, however, insists that dialogue is not the same as negotiation. Neither will the process of dialogue include people who were involved in the failed coup of May 2015.

In terms of openness of the current government, the government put the international community as well as diplomatic missions in Burundi on notice that they should state clearly whether they recognize the current government or not. If one country makes it clear that it supports and recognizes the current government, meetings for diplomats or foreign government officials at any level of the country's leadership will be made easier. Some information about a plan to kill the president and some highly positioned leaders has been circulated, explaining why there are restrictions on who can see the president.

Some good initiatives have been taken by the government. A group of teenagers who were caught during the protests as well as some people arrested during the Kayanza attacks are or have been attending civic education training workshops in Rumonge. After their training is complete, they will be sent back home, where, it is hoped, they will make positive contributions to their communities.

The first group made of underage prisoners has been released and the Red Cross was in charge of bringing them back to their families. This civic education program will continue and needs to be supported.

For adults who are going through trials because of their involvement in the protests, coup, and armed group attacks, there is a window of opportunity for amnesty, but this necessarily will happen after their trials are complete, as a matter of due process.

Finally, the government has pointed out that people working in embassies and other diplomatic missions do not even go to the suburbs of Bujumbura, in order to inquire what the reality on the ground is. This has resulted in many statements being made based on faulty or biased information. The government has issued strong requests that all people involved in the process of addressing the current crisis to visit the whole country and to see how differently the suburbs of Bujumbura look in comparison to other areas, if they wish to write accurate reports on Burundi.

Views of the opposition

Despite the fact that I was unable to meet with the leaders of the opposition in Burundi, I had interesting and informative conversations with members of opposition groups and political parties. It was explained to me that the major motivation to fight is unequal opportunities that were given to former fighters. While some people were demobilized, another group was left alone even if they were promised to be called later; it appeared that no one cared about them after all.

I heard that the rebellion has structures and that it has members from all ethnic groups and includes youth from some suburbs of Bujumbura who were trained during or after protests. I learned that there is close collaboration with some security forces currently active within the government.

One opposition member I met said that, reflecting on his life experience, he is convinced that, no matter what negotiations come up with, he will not hand his gun back, unless he is properly demobilized because he was lied too many times and he wants to see his life and the life of his family back on track with good economic standing. He still complains about the fact that he and some of his colleagues received nothing more than tennis shoes and a radio as demobilization package. He concludes that his colleague in the field will not accept any decision from the negotiation, because they want to have a representative to the negotiation whose holds, at the very least, the rank of lieutenant.

Religious leaders, civil society, and educational institutions

Religious leaders, especially the Catholic Church have noticed that it is not easy for them to operate in an environment in which they announced publicly their opposition to President Nkurunziza's third term. As damage control, they are calling both parties to dialogue without pushing too hard. They are also trying to cope with the current situation and regain trust because it is the only way they can have their word listened to by both the government and the opposition.

Civil society operates under fear. There are some facts that cannot be addressed in the near future and, therefore, instead of taking extreme positions, those operating in Burundi try to cope with the situation and report with more nuanced analysis to the extent that they can. Civil society requests the government to stop immediately acts of harassment, intimidation and arbitrary detention against members of civil society organizations, journalists and other human right activists and peacebuilders, as well as members of their families carrying out their activities in a risky environment.Burundian civil society would like to see the establishment of an independent and rigorous inquiry in order to establish responsibility for the violence observed in Burundi since April 2015 and apply any criminal, civil or administrative sanctions applicable under the law

Conditions in educational institutions at every level have deteriorated and may continue to get worse if no urgent support is brought to the country. People I talked to in education unanimously agreed to the following:

There is a general absence of highly educated people in Burundian politics. This may have been due to the many years of civil war, destruction of education facilities, death of experienced educators, and use of force by students to get good grades instead of getting them based on merit. This was noticed in many schools, where instructors were killed or forced to allow students to graduate even when the students did not fulfill the course requirements. The other component is that, many people got positions because they fought the war militarily and this was a reward for the efforts they made in the bush, even if they were not otherwise qualified to do the job.

The other major problem is the new education system Bachelor—Masters- Doctorate (LMD, or Licence, Maitrise, Doctorat) which was launched with insufficient studies in term of implementation and transition from the previous system. People in education leadership with whom I spoke were desperate and shared with me the complexity of the situation. They are not very sure where students graduating from the ninth grade will go, they worry that the country does not have instructors who can teach courses such as art, music, and drawing, among other teacher shortages.

Some week-long basic workshops were conducted to equip educators with skills to teach new courses such as English, Swahili, Music, and Arts. Educators themselves testify, however, that they still did not learn enough to allow them to teach those courses adequately.

Finally, some school principals who were dismissed from their leadership position and demoted to teach as basic instructors with the new system, prefer to abandon the job entirely. This has put education in a dire situation.

I personally see the deteriorating education system as a real threat to security in Burundi. If young people do not have access to good education—and consequently to good jobs later—no matter how hard we work to address the current issues, violence will never cease. It is a good thing to call for investments and job creation in Burundi to hire thousands of educated and non-educated youth, but this will only provide "negative peace" insofar as we will not have put in place structures that guarantee better education for all in Burundi.

The role of neighboring countries

Throughout the history, Burundi and Rwanda have been following the same trajectory. They either engage in peace together or they get in trouble at the same time. Courageous analysts have denounced the negative role that Rwanda has been playing in the current crisis in Burundi. It was not until President Kagame, announced it publicly that the international community started to see how Rwanda has an active role in the Burundi crisis. Hopefully, Rwanda will be soon pressured to abandon that strategy. Other countries also such as Tanzania, Democratic Republic of the Congo and Uganda have a major role in stopping current violence. I am convinced that if all the leaders of the region commit themselves to the cause for peace in Burundi and talk to all the parties in conflict in Burundi through unofficial ways, the current issue will be addressed soon. The problem is that some actors want to use the force and pressure as well as "rule of law" as way to address the conflict. Unless we understand that a gun makes stronger a gunman and that humble and smooth approach to the gunman can convince him to put down his weapon before innocent lives are lost, we will not address the current Burundi conflict.

Recommended actions

I have several recommendations for actions on the part of the international community, including Burundi's partners in the United States and other countries.

First, we need to improve the economy (job creation, investment and opportunities for youth and other people who are able to work). A big investment plan, not necessarily like the Marshall Plan but sized to fit Burundi's specific needs, will not only promote sustainable peace and security in the country, but will also improve the stability of the region as a whole.

The United States should invest in that small country, because even if it does not have the natural resources equivalent to the DRC or Angola, its high number of active men and women can either be a real asset to grow the economy or they can be a real threat to the region and to the world, if joining terrorist or rebel groups offers better pay and opportunities. The announcement that Burundi will be excluded from AGOA is troublesome in this regard, as well as the fact that competing countries in the region are open to U.S. (and other foreign) investment and may snatch opportunities from Burundi's hands in a way that is not beneficial to the entire region, economically or politically.

Second, we should improve education programs (both long- and short-term with regard to peace education). The long term would improve people's thinking as well as providing leaders who are highly educated, sparking well-strategized leadership and innovative ideologies. We need to make sure the new education model (LMD) is supported sufficiently and experts are sent to Burundi to do capacity building in teaching some courses such as English, art, Swahili, and so forth.

PTSD is a continuing problem in Burundi, so, third, we need to create a substantial program of trauma healing that would be implemented nationwide. This should incorporate a new type of trauma healing approach that would have different layers of activities depending on the roles and responsibilities each person has. The same program should be in some ways included in the peace education curriculum that is needed in schools.

This would also include nonviolence activities and teachings. For several generations, the Burundian people have considered violence as the only alternative to deliver themselves and to help them reach their goals. If new generations are not taught that nonviolence can play a major role in the transformation of systems as well as helping people reach their goals peacefully, it will still be hard for them to reach sustainable peace.

Some other suggestions:

1. Help the government disarm all militias regardless of political affiliation
2. Request the government to restore the freedom of expression, allowing private media (newspapers and radio) to re-open
3. Allow civil society to operate freely and without fear of being arrested and re-open soon their bank accounts that have been frozen for investigation purposes. This goes along with training of civil society personnel and journalists to improve their capacity for reporting and acting responsibly
4. Start extensive campaigns calling refugees to return to Burundi because they are living in inhumane conditions in camps, where the information they get is mostly is biased by political views which overly dramatize the situation in Burundi
5. Strengthen the African Union's human rights observers and require them to have toll-free phones to allow every Burundian to reach them and report misconduct
6. Urge the Burundian government to have conflict resolution experts working with the National Commission for Dialogue, to focus on long-term goals and sustainability of peace in Burundi
7. Sternly urge the Rwandan government not to continue its interference in the Burundian crisis and, if necessary, put in place some sanctions against Rwanda

Mr. Chairman and members of the subcommittee, I thank you for this opportunity to speak to you today and I will be happy to answer any questions you have and to engage in a productive and informative discussion with my fellow witnesses.

Senator FLAKE. Thank you.

Thank you again for the testimony.

We have been joined by the ranking member, Senator Cardin. So let me ask a few questions before turning to him.

Mr. Siegle, in your prepared remarks, you mentioned that part of what might have motivated Nkurunziza to run for reelection is people encouraging him to move away from the Arusha Accords, as they seem to be too harsh on the Hutus here.

If that is the case, moving back to the Arusha Accords, is that going to satisfy the president and his followers? Or will the same underlying problems as they see them remain, that this accord is too restrictive on their rights?

Dr. SIEGLE. Well, I think absolutely that is the central issue here. What we have seen really is a split within the ruling party, the CNDD–FDD.

As with most of the major political parties in Burundi, since Arusha, there has been a commitment to a multiethnic coalition-building approach to politics. That is why there was some hope that we would see a genuine transition this year.

But I think it has been, over the last year especially that hardliners in the CNDD–FDD have resisted that transition. They do see an opportunity to break out of Arusha, which through ethnic quotas has limited the influence that Hutus can have, and they feel that that is their rightful position to have greater influence within the party and outside.

So I think that is exactly what they are hoping for. They want to break Arusha. They want the third term, and then rewrite the political rules under the auspices of some sort of national dialogue and that way be in a much stronger position for a hard-line Hutu position.

So I think absolutely they will be resistant to moving back to Arusha.

Senator FLAKE. Mr. Vircoulon, you mentioned that the regional spillover conflict is not just a threat, it is now a reality. Can you talk more about that in terms of refugees and other issues, in terms of the regional aspect of this crisis?

Mr. VIRCOULON. Thank you, Chairman.

Indeed, as we sit, there are more than 200,000 refugees in basically 9 months, Burundians who fled their country. Most of them are in western Tanzania. About 70,000 of them are in Rwanda. The rest are between eastern Congo and Uganda.

What we have seen since the beginning of this refugee crisis is, of course, some cross-border security problems that have increased with Rwanda, also with the Democratic Republic of Congo. As it has been said previously, there have been some credible reports about recruitment in the refugee camps. So those are security problems that have already emerged because of the refugee crisis.

Of course, there are also some very serious humanitarian problems. There was an outbreak of cholera in western Tanzania in June and July that was fortunately contained by the humanitarian NGOs. But as the flow of refugees is going to increase, we are likely to see these kinds of epidemics start again in western Tanzania and also probably in south.

The other very important humanitarian problem that I must mention is food and security. Burundi is a country that has been suffering from food insecurity for a long time now. With this crisis, agricultural production is declining in the country. There are reports by humanitarian organizations that the people have more and more troubles in the countryside to find food. So I think the World Food Program is already making a contingency plan for that.

Senator FLAKE. Mr. Nimuraba, you had mentioned that you would not advocate sanctions against the regime. Does that include travel sanctions against members of the regime or economic sanctions? What are you particularly warning against?

Mr. NIMURABA. I say that because sanctions really do not have any impact, because people who are targeted rarely travel. That is first. And second, when you approach somebody with sanctions, you do not approach him. You kind of put a barrier between the person and yourself. Then people either from the opposition or from the government will be less likely to get involved in any kind of dialogue or conversation to find a common way, because once somebody is already targeted, he will try to protect himself.

As you can see in the Burundian history, many people have been accused of many kinds of mass atrocities and killings and human rights violations who have been protecting themselves. Some of the problems that we are facing come from that aspect; people try to protect themselves. The more we put pressure on them and add more sanctions, the more they will strengthen their contentious tactics and keep more people around them to make sure they are strong and safe enough to resist any kind of invasion or attack from outside.

Senator FLAKE. Thank you.

Dr. Siegle, I asked Assistant Secretary Thomas-Greenfield about the tipping point between political struggle and pure ethnic conflict. When will we hit that tipping point? What are the warning signs we ought to look for?

Dr. SIEGLE. Well, I think that is the tension that we are facing. And I think as Assistant Secretary Thomas-Greenfield mentioned, one of the noteworthy observations about what has happened so far is the degree to which Burundian society has largely resisted going down that path.

Senator FLAKE. It is always underlying.

Dr. SIEGLE. Not only that, but I think the government has actively tried to play it up. But I think it is important from an external engagement standpoint to recognize that many people in the opposition, including CNARED, the political alliance that has been created out of Addis Ababa, they are mostly Hutu. These are people who were prominent within the CNDD–FDD.

To the extent that the political opposition is seen as being multiethnic, it can help defuse the impulse to break down into those ethnic groupings.

So I think the question will be to what extent do the region's international actors appear that they are going to help be a part of this process, so that in the end people on the ground do not feel that they have to revert back into those categorizations.

Senator FLAKE. Thank you.

Senator Cardin?

Senator CARDIN. First, I want to thank Senator Flake for calling this hearing. I guess most Americans would have a hard time finding Burundi on the map, but what is happening there is of great concern. I think this hearing is extremely important, so that we understand that there are people at risk every day, and the numbers are growing.

We put a great deal of confidence in the Arusha Accords because it dealt with some of the fundamental problems of the country—constitutional reform, protecting the rights of the minority, dealing with proper representation within the military, limitations on terms of the president. The international community felt that those provisions were the framework for long-term peace in the country.

There are lots of challenges, as you all point out. I understand the concern about sanctions. But there is also a concern that if there are no penalties that you just encourage that type of horrible conduct.

We never want to jeopardize the delivery of humanitarian assistance. So we never look at those areas, but we do look at matters that can be empowering corruption to make sure that we do not encourage that.

I guess my question is, I was very disturbed, Mr. Siegle, when you said that the president's desire to run for a third term was in a way an attempt to undo the Arusha Accords. Of course, after that, he then instituted many repressive practices within the country, taking away the rights of many of the people of the region. Now if he is rewarded by the reconfiguration of the Arusha Accords, it seems to me that is not the way we move forward.

So I am trying to figure out how we bring about peace for Burundi, protecting the integrity of what was behind the Arusha Accords, so at the end of the day, those who are responsible for the atrocities are not rewarded and there is some hope for long-term stability in the country.

Try to give me a roadmap as to how you see us moving forward. What has happened has happened. I for one do not want to give up on the Arusha Accords.

What are the most important immediate steps to be taken to end the risk factors for the population and to get us back into a framework where we can have a lasting peace in the country? Give me your priorities. What are the first two or three things we have to do?

Dr. SIEGLE. I will start, and then I am sure my copanelists will want add in.

I think what we want to be doing is both offering a roadmap as well as putting pressure on the government. I think it is clearly evident over the past——

Senator CARDIN. And the roadmap is not the Arusha Accords or it is?

Dr. SIEGLE. Arusha is the framework. I think when I talk about roadmap, it is how to get back to Arusha. So Arusha is the goal. It is the framework. We have veered off of that, so how do you get back on to that?

It is clear, with all the decisions that Mr. Nkurunziza and his allies have made over the last 9 months, that they are willing to take the country down the tubes in order to try to retain their hold on power, so they are only going to respond to strong pressure.

Senator CARDIN. So what is that strong pressure?

Dr. SIEGLE. I think there are several things. First is I think we do need to more actively support a move toward a transitional government that the current Burundian Government does not see as a focal point for the political dialogue in Burundi. We have seen in Burkina Faso, in Mali, in Guinea, that there needs to be a technocratic-based political government comprising all parties whose goal it will be to bring us back to a point of elections that will allow for a resumption——

Senator CARDIN. I follow that, but what pressure can the international community bring to bear to cause the government to move in that direction?

Dr. SIEGLE. There are a couple of other things that I would put out there.

One is a push for a peacekeeping force. We were talking about this in the earlier panel, a potential Chapter VII mandate for a peacekeeping force to go into Burundi. I think, again, if the regional international community demonstrates enough commitment, that force would not have to be a peace enforcement force. I think they could be sent in as peacekeepers to keep the sides away from each other.

I think it is important to keep in mind that the conflict in Burundi right now is not a typical conflict of two organized armed factions. These are hit-and-run types of attacks, assassinations.

So an early, strong international military presence can help provide a buffering influence. It will then also isolate the Burundian Government.

I think the role of the ICC is important here, too. We already saw with the open letter sent by the ICC prosecutor indicating that actions taken in Burundi, the inflammatory language that was being used, would be highly scrutinized and be used as evidence in any subsequent ICC investigation.

I think by making that clear, that there are going to be costs to be paid, it will be another way of exerting pressure.

Mr. NIMURABA. Thank you. With respect to everybody's analysis, I would like to say that I strongly disagree with this idea of having a transitional government, because if you see how the current government has been trying to work kind of work hard to keep the power of the country even when the situation was not easy, I do not think this idea of a transitional government would work; suggesting transitional government may bring back another civil war and this war may be worse than what we are seeing now.

For me, a good approach is first started by us. What we do is to change the approach as I said not to issue a statement, but to go in a kind of nice way to request, "We really need A, B, C from you, the government."

Those kinds of requests that we bring to the government can include asking the government to integrate people from the opposition. We have many people in Rwanda and everywhere who are really strong leaders, if we can negotiate with them in a nice way. We are dealing with people who have been fighting for more than 20 years, and many have post-traumatic stress disorder or something like that. We need to make sure we understand that.

If we approach them in a nice way and then request them to do some kind of concessions, that will allow us not only to have those people fearing for their security to come back to Burundi and also to be integrated into the government. That would really reduce the tensions. That is one side.

For the other side, I talked to people who are fighting. The major concern for them is to be able to survive economically. Along that line of effort, if we have some kind of economic incentive to bring them to work and to give them some kind of job that would motivate them to abandon violence practices and contribute to peace, development and nation building.

But if you see how hard the positions are, I do not think any transition will really work. Thank you.

Senator CARDIN. Mr. Vircoulon?

Mr. VIRCOULON. Senator, in terms of priority action, I think the dialogue, the international dialogue is very important and this dialogue must be an opportunity to discuss the Arusha agreement. I can elaborate on that later.

Senator CARDIN. Dialogue for the purposes of modifying?

Mr. VIRCOULON. Of making some adjustments and changes. I think the Arusha agreement, indeed, has been the stumbling block of peace and of the new regime. But I have been in conversations with the people from the ruling party over the past 5 years and they have always been very clear. Their view has always been very clear about the fact that this is now a 15-year-old peace agreement and the political situation has changed in the country. So they always wanted to make some adjustments.

I think that sometimes conflict starts because a conversation does not happen. Actually, what I think has been missing in Burundi over the past 5 years is that conversation about the Arusha agreement. I think if we want to have lasting peace in Burundi, we have to facilitate this discussion and find middle ground between those who want to make changes and adjustments to the Arusha agreement and those who want to keep it.

It is clear that there are some key principles in the Arusha agreement that must not be changed. I think that probably the most important provisions in the Arusha agreement are those that have not been implemented. I am thinking about the logistics provision of the Arusha agreement because the provisional—I mean, a lot of political leaders in Burundi now, and I think it is very important to know that, benefit from provisional amnesty and, therefore, the crimes of the civil war have never been addressed.

I fully agree with the idea of a peacekeeping force and the planning for a peacekeeping force. MINUSCO, the largest peacekeeping force in the world, is just at the border of Burundi. Of course, the U.S. Government can help to identify those who are responsible for the violence and adopt some targeted sanctions.

But I think there is leverage that is at this stage very important. It is the participation of the Burundian army to the mission in Somalia. I think this is a very important leverage, given the number of troops and given the financial support that Burundi gets for that mission. I think this leverage should also be used.

Senator CARDIN. Thank you. Thank you all very much.

Thank you, Mr. Chairman.

Senator FLAKE. Mr. Vircoulon, talking again about the regional aspect of this, is the United States playing a constructive role in making sure that this does not spill over any further in the region? If not, what more could we be doing?

Mr. VIRCOULON. I think the United States has been quick to look at the situation in Burundi. Unfortunately, I think some of the statements that were made at the beginning of this year by the United States should have been made a bit earlier.

But now I think it is very important that the administration keeps talking to all the stakeholders in the region and I think keeps helping the African Union to be in charge of the mediation.

There is clearly a diplomatic impasse at the moment between the African Union and the East African Community. As it was said, President Museveni is in charge of the mediation, but this mediation does not seem to go anywhere. But there is still a reluctance, actually, to transfer the mediation.

I think the United States should advise and help with the transfer of that mediation from President Museveni to the African Union. As I said, I think it is better to have a collective mediation led by the African Union.

But it is clear that, on the diplomatic side, the United States can help convince some stakeholders to transfer the mediation from President Museveni to the African Union.

Senator FLAKE. Let me just drill down a little further, when you are talking about going back into the Arusha Accords and adjusting, it can be really only the 60/40 kind of split. Is that what you are talking about? Or the term limits on the president? What aspects of the Arusha Accords are most critical to adjust, in terms of the ruling party? Are those the two items that they are really concerned about?

Mr. VIRCOULON. Well, I think they are very concerned about the fact that you have that 60/40 percentage rule, indeed, but also the 50/50 percent rule in the security forces. We must remember that actually some counting has been done recently concerning the number of Hutu and Tutsis in the security services. It indicates maybe the warning signs you were referring to earlier about the ethnic dimension of that conflict.

So it is a very important, I think, to address those issues and not just to push them aside and think that they must not be taken into consideration. It has been a very long-term claim by the CNDD–FDD rulers to review that agreement, and they tried to do it with a constitutional review in 2014 and did not manage to do it.

So I think instead of them dismantling the accord, which is what they have started doing for many years—and we wrote a report in 2012 that was titled "Bye-Bye Arusha?" to explain the process. So instead of having them dismantle the accord de facto and trying to impose a constitutional review next year, I think it would be much better to have a discussion to reach a consensus about what must be adjusted and changed in this agreement.

Of course, this can only be decided by the Burundian stakeholders themselves. So I think the role of the international community should just be to facilitate this discussion.

Senator FLAKE. Dr. Siegle, do you have any thoughts on that?

Dr. SIEGLE. I do. First, I would reiterate that the commitment to Arusha was actually quite strong within the CNDD–FDD, and there were 130 senior officials within the party who wrote a petition to Nkurunziza in April requesting that he not seek a third term and that he respect the terms of the Arusha Accords.

So when we talk about people wanting to break out of Arusha, it is not the entire party. It is the remnants of the CNDD–FDD. It is the hardliners that want this. We have to recall that even back into the early stages of the negotiation in the 2000s, there were members and entities within the CNDD–FDD that did not want to sign. They were late in signing. So there has always been resistance. That will continue to be there.

But I think within Burundi society writ large, there is actually quite a lot of pride in the Arusha Accords. It has provided them a pathway for a multiethnic democratic society, and we see that within the political sphere. We see that within civil society. We see it within the military, which has made great progress in moving toward a multiethnic and professional force.

So I think, by and large, the benchmark within Burundi society more generally is very supportive of Arusha, and they see this as a way to move past the ethnic politics of the past.

I do think that there is concern when we talk about reopening Arusha. That is exactly what the government will want to do. It is, I think, a very clever negotiating tactic. "Let us have a national dialogue. Let us talk about things we need change." And the real goal there is to water down these terms that have helped move the country forward.

I would add to what Thierry mentioned. In addition to the justice sector, one of the major flaws, one of the things missing in Arusha, was the police, the intelligence services, the gendarmerie were not included, so they have remained politicized. Those are the mechanisms that the government has used to try to push forward its political agenda.

Senator FLAKE. Yes, Thierry?

Mr. VIRCOULON. Chairman, indeed, I can only agree with Dr. Siegal. The whole CNDD–FDD party was not against the Arusha agreement. I think the problem now is that most of the moderates have left the ruling party. Those who are in control of the party now are opposed to the Arusha agreement and its principles.

I do not want any misinterpretations or misunderstandings about what I said previously. I think it is important to have the discussion about the Burundians, and the discussion about the Arusha agreement, that they did not have really before. I think, of course, it must be done in a consensual way. And the outcome of the discussion must be, of course, a consensus among all the stakeholders.

I think the CNDD–FDD rulers have mentioned that they were not at the negotiation table when the accord was negotiated between 1996 and 2000. Therefore, that is very often the reason why they say they were not part of that negotiation and we do not like some of the provisions of the accords.

So this must be taken into consideration, if we want to have a substantial dialogue about this crisis in Burundi.

Senator FLAKE. Thank you.

Yes?

Mr. NIMURABA. Thank you. I think there are some kinds of issues that we do not discuss but which are really more important, because when we try to deal with the current issue, we need to see where we are and the kind of forces we are facing.

Coming back to the Arusha Accords, I think it is clear that I do not ignore the kind of manipulations that have taken place for the past year, but the issue was not of the Arusha Accords, but the interpretation of the Arusha Accords in terms of terms. If the opposition and the ruling party agree on several aspects of the Arusha Accords, the only issue was the interpretation.

The problem started, when the constitutional court decided that President Nkurunnziza had the right to run for another term. The understanding of the Constitution remains the main issue. Now we need to see how to move forward with that aspect. Thank you.

Senator FLAKE. Thank you.

I appreciate the testimony that has been given. This will help us as we formulate policy and move forward and work with the State Department and the administration on U.S. policy toward Burundi and the region. So I appreciate it.

For the purposes of members and their staff here, the record will remain open until the close of business on Friday, including for members to submit questions for the record.

So as they submit these questions, if you could answer promptly, that would be appreciated. That will be part of the record.

Senator FLAKE. With the thanks of the committee, the committee stands adjourned.

[Whereupon, at 4:08 p.m., the hearing was adjourned.]

ADDITIONAL MATERIAL SUBMITTED FOR THE RECORD

RESPONSES TO QUESTIONS FOR THE RECORD SUBMITTED TO ASSISTANT SECRETARY LINDA THOMAS-GREENFIELD BY SENATOR BENJAMIN L. CARDIN

Question. Last week, U.S. Special Envoy to the Great Lakes Tom Perriello stated that Burundi "is facing a real possibility of civil war." What concrete contingency plans have the region and the rest of the international community made to respond to the outbreak of conflict?

Answer. The United States has encouraged the African Union to undertake contingency planning efforts, and we have been in contact with other likeminded partners concerning the need for a coordinated response in the event the crisis in Burundi devolves into a civil war. We are also encouraging the United Nations to work with the African Union on contingency planning.

Question. On December 5, a New York Times article suggested that opposition members are stepping up attacks on the government to cast the government in a bad light, and pressure it to engage in dialogue. Have the international community's diplomatic efforts provided a perverse incentive for violence from the opposition?

Answer. We have consistently condemned all violence, whether committed by government or non-government actors, and called upon all stakeholders to commit without preconditions to participating in internationally-mediated talks. We remain convinced that an inclusive and internationally-mediated dialogue provides the best route for reaching a consensual and sustainable solution to this crisis. UN and AU statements have similarly condemned all parties whose actions have undermined the peace and stability of Burundi. The sanctions regimes imposed by the United States and European Union have named both government and opposition actors, all of whom have been involved in either government-sponsored violence against the civilian population and other human rights abuses, involvement in the coup attempt in May 2015, or involvement in supporting violent anti-government acts in Burundi since the coup. We will continue to work with our international partners to press all parties to refrain from violence, and to commit to serious engagement in the internationally mediated dialogue, the ultimate objective is which is to develop a consensus path forward to return Burundi to the path of stability and peace it was on before President Nkurunziza opted to pursue a third term in office contrary to the provisions of the Arusha Peace and Reconciliation Agreement that ended the Burundian civil war.

Question. The same New York Times report mentions claims by people on the ground that they are part of a resistance movement called the "Abajeune." Are we aware of a youth wing of the armed opposition, and what does its existence portend as relates to the security situation on the ground?

Answer. There are multiple anti-Nkurunziza armed groups. The Abajeune developed as a general term for young people involved in demonstrations against the government; it is not, to our knowledge, the name of a specific armed group. The Abajeune are, however, primary targets for recruitment into the multiple anti-Nkurunziza armed groups. The most obvious armed group recruiting Abajeune is the Movement for Solidarity and Democracy (MSD) headed by Alexis Sinduhije. Many members of the Abajeune are compensated by the anti-Nkurunziza opposition for their activities, a particular enticement as most were unemployed before being recruited by opposition groups and becoming involved in anti-government demonstrations.

The ruling party, the CNDD-FDD, has a youth wing known as the Imbonerakure that also has been known to arm some of its members. To the extent that young men are readily persuaded to engage in violence, their recruitment by both the ruling party and by opposition groups will make it even more difficult to restore stability to Burundi.

Question. The East African Community has designated Ugandan President Yoweri Museveni as the point man to end the current political crisis, but progress has been slow. The late Howard Wolpe, who served as Chair of the Africa subcommittee in the House, and who also served as Great Lakes Special Envoy, wrote in 2011 about previous regional efforts to bring about peace in Burundi, "With the benefit of hindsighta it appears that regional sponsorship of the Burundi peace process was not an unmitigated blessing. The belligerent parties saw several of the regional states as partisans of one side or the other and were therefore less inclined to trust the neutrality and professionalism of the regionally sponsored facilitation."

Is there mistrust of the Ugandans and/or Rwandans by Burundian actors? If not, why haven't the talks commenced? What is the international plan to overcome objections of the parties to a dialogue?

Burundi is reportedly due to take over as chair of the East African Commission at the next Heads of State summit and lead the organization for the next year. What is the EAC's intention with regards to the rotation? What impact will it have on diplomatic efforts?

Answer. We have conducted extensive outreach at the highest levels around the region, and inside Burundi, urging the immediate start of an internationally-mediated dialogue. The recent dramatic increase in the levels of violence have underscored the urgency in starting the dialogue, but distrust among the regional states remains a challenge to the success and legitimacy of the Ugandan-led dialogue. Special Envoy Perriello and the other members of the international Great Lakes Envoy team have offered to observe the dialogue, as the international community has done during previous peace processes. We continue to work closely with the AU and regional heads of state to ensure that the parties come to the table willing to engage in serious dialogue aimed at putting Burundi back on the path toward stability that the Arusha Peace and Reconciliation Agreement ushers in over a decade ago. Opposition members have now stated their readiness to come to the table without preconditions. We are working with the region to pressure President Nkurunziza to ensure high-level participation by the government throughout the process.

Burundi is scheduled to take the chair of the East African Community (EAC) in 2016. Tanzania is the current chair of the EAC. While civil society organizations in East Africa have called for Burundi not to assume the chair until it resolves its political and human rights crisis, the EAC has not taken any action concerning the chairmanship. Any decision concerning the chairmanship will be made at the next summit of the EAC heads of state, which will take place in early 2016.

Question. On October 17, the African Union (AU) Peace and Security Council issued a communique which asked the AU Commission to ensure that Burundian "members of the defense and security forces involved in human rights violations and other acts of violence do not take part in AU-led peace support operations." Five thousand of the 20,000 troops in the AU mission in Somalia are Burundian. What is our contingency plan if we find—for whatever reason— the Burundian contingent must be pulled out of Somalia?

Answer. AMISOM, the peacekeeping mission in Somalia, is organized and led by the AU. If AU member states decide to pull out the Burundian contingents in AMISOM, we would encourage other capable countries to fill in the gap. The AU leadership is seized with this issue.

Question. The AU Commission deployed human rights monitors and military experts to Bujumbura to "monitor the human rights situation on the ground and report violations of human rights and international humanitarian law, and to verify, in collaboration with the Government of Burundi and other concerned actors, the process of disarming the militias and other armed groups, respectively." The AU Peace and Security Council asked that the number of monitors and military expects be increased, and appealed for additional resources to support their mandate.

What is the status of the agreement between the AU and the government of Burundi on deployment of human rights monitors and military observers? Are they able to fulfill their mandate both within and outside the capital? What will their mobility accomplish and how will this further regional aims?

Have we made any contribution to support the deployment? What else are we doing to assist with efforts to put in place mechanisms for accountability?

Are monitors collecting evidence and documenting abuses for possible prosecution?

Answer. The human rights monitors and military observers are in Bujumbura, but there have been numerous delays by the Burundian government in permitting them to begin their work, including the government's demand that a memorandum of understanding (MOU) be concluded with the AU. While the MOU remains unsigned, the AU informs us that the monitors are able to perform at least some of their mandated duties and have reported on the deteriorating security and humanitarian situation in Bujumbura and the surrounding areas. The security situation on the ground in Burundi also prevents the monitors from moving outside of the capital.

In addition to the sanctions announced on November 23, we are prepared to consider additional sanctions in an effort to hold accountable those responsible for exacerbating the crisis and committing violations of human rights. We support the EU's sanction regime and the African Union's consideration of sanctions.

Furthermore, USAID is currently providing funding to the Office of the United Nations High Commissioner for Human Rights for its Burundi Country Office to allow them to fulfill their mission to monitor human rights. This is an additional mechanism to the work of the AU team.

Question. We have spent at least $200 million training and equipping the Burundian military for deployment in AMISOM, MINUSCA, and for counterterrorism efforts. And yet we have spent no money to support democracy and governance activities in the past several years.

Why haven't we invested in democracy and governance programs in Burundi?

To your knowledge, have we ever supported accountability efforts, grassroots reconciliation or democracy and governance programs in Burundi? What have such programs achieved?

Answer. The U.S. government has supported and continues to support democracy, human rights and governance programs (DRG) across Burundi. USAID has a long history of supporting reconciliation programs responding to the aftermath of the civil war as well as other potential emerging drivers of conflict, including land disputes. USAID is also engaged in advancing respect for human rights and monitoring human rights violations throughout Burundi. The focus on the possibility of atrocities in the run up to the 2015 elections prompted an increase starting in 2013 in DRG and other resources for activities in Burundi.

USAID funds programs to promote grassroots reconciliation, reduce the potential for conflict, and promote human rights. Through these, the United States supports conflict mitigation and resolution programs focused on youth and other potential conflict drivers. These programs aim to create a space for constructive dialogue between political and civil society leaders and encourage collaborative youth participation in problem-solving, community development, and reconciliation activities within their communities.

USAID previously provided support to the Ministry of Good Governance through the Burundi Policy Reform program, providing technical and material assistance to the Ministry in the planning and launch of the government-wide accountability in public administration campaign. This program also worked with women leaders and provided technical assistance to the process of revising the land code. Accountability and transparency were strengthened through support for the development of a communication strategy to inform citizens, taxpayers, stakeholders, and employees of why the Burundi Revenue Authority was created; how it would perform its duties effectively; and, how it would solicit feedback from customers and response to their concerns.

We have engaged many times with members of the government, civil society, and victims' organizations to craft credible mechanisms and approaches to address Burundi's legacy of mass atrocities, promote accountability, and engender reconciliation. True accountability often means shining a light in dark places and uncovering truths many would prefer to leave alone. However, we are also aware that if the legacy of mass atrocities is not addressed in a way that allows societies to seek justice and to address the root causes of violence, there is a high risk of repeating the violations and abuses of the past.

Question. On November 23, the President issued an Executive Order which imposed sanctions of four individuals who were deemed to have taken actions that, among other things, threaten the peace, security or stability of Burundi.

What do we expect our sanctions to accomplish?

Did we collaborate with the European Union, or the African Union on determining when to impose the sanctions, and upon whom we imposed them? Would such collective action have a significant impact?

Answer. Executive Order 13712, signed by President Obama on November 23, is a signal that there are serious consequences for anyone, whether in the government or the opposition, who exacerbates the crisis by promoting violence. We will continue to assess the application of sanctions to other individuals, including anyone found to be providing support to individuals already listed.

We supported the EU's early use of sanctions, and are in regular contact with them about next steps to support a resolution of this conflict. We have commended the AU's threat of sanctions and welcome the continued consideration of AU sanctions, which would have particular weight as they could restrict the ability of sanctioned individuals to travel within the region.

Question. In recent months, there have been widespread reports of fragmentation and desertions within the military. There have also been concerns that Burundian soldiers deployed to the AMISOM mission in Somalia have gone for months without pay. Some analysts are concerned that the return of 5000 disgruntled soldiers from Somalia could lead to the further deterioration of the situation on the ground.

Where are deserting soldiers going and what effect do we expect the desertion to have on the security situation?

Are Burundian soldiers being consistently paid by the government?

Answer. While the Burundian military is still one of the more professional institutions in the country, the ongoing crisis is reportedly affecting the morale of many soldiers, especially those currently deployed outside Burundi. There are also increasing reports of the ruling party (the National Council for the Defense of Democracy, Forces for the Defense of Democracy, or CNDD-FDD) using the relatively undisciplined and untrained Imbonerakure militia as part of the country's deployed force to Somalia alongside police and military, which further impacts the morale of professional soldiers. We are seeing increasing reports of desertions and would expect this trend to continue, with some deserters possibly joining the armed insurgency, and others becoming either refugees in neighboring countries or internally displaced persons. Donors have cut considerable assistance to the Burundian government since the start of the crisis in April, and the rising conflict has sent the local economy into freefall. The Burundian government is running out of cash on hand, and it is uncertain how long it can continue to pay the salaries of not just its security forces, but other civil servants as well. To date, we have received conflicting reports regarding the payment of salaries to members of the military, an issue we are consistently tracking.

RESPONSES TO QUESTIONS FOR THE RECORD SUBMITTED TO SIXTE VIGNY NIMURABA BY SENATOR BENJAMIN L. CARDIN

Question. There has been more than one documented instance of ethnically-based mass killings in Burundi since independence. Hundreds of thousands have been murdered in systematic, deliberate attacks based on ethnicity going back over 40 years. Article 8 of the 2000 Arusha Accords calls for a National Truth and Reconciliation Commission to be established. A draft law for the TRC's establishment was not even submitted until 2011.

What is the status of the Commission, and how has the delay affected reconciliation in Burundi?

Answer. The Truth and Reconciliation Commission was finally established on December 4, 2014. Its mission is to investigate and establish the truth about the serious violations of human rights and international humanitarian law committed during the period from the date of independence on July 1, 1962 until December 4, 2008, the date marking the end of the period of belligerence.

However, the Commission faces several problems. All of its members were appointed by the President and are from the ruling CNDD-FDD party. Opposition parties boycotted the entire process. The law establishing this Commission omitted the judicial provisions created by the Arusha Agreement and instead stressed forgiveness as a basis for its work. This undermined the goal of establishing responsibility as a basis to root out impunity as required by the Arusha Accords. The law includes no provision for protection of witnesses but instead threatens them with punishment if they give false testimony. Furthermore, a 2004 law blocked dissemination of the final TRC report. The main effect of these weaknesses in the establishment of the TRC is to reinforce an attitude of impunity that remains deeply embedded in the culture of Burundian political leaders.

Consistent with the political nature of the conflict in Burundi, the issue of inter-communal reconciliation is seen as less urgent as there is a general openness of Hutus and Tutsis to live together cooperatively. Even now, despite the attempts by hardline elements of the CNDD-FDD to stir up ethnic animosities, there is not an intrinsic hatred between groups.

Question. Is the current political turmoil in part a result of this delay?

Answer. Delays in establishing the Truth and Reconciliation Commission have contributed to the current crisis—more by reinforcing the perception of impunity rather than by fostering a lack of reconciliation among ordinary Burundians, however. This Commission was established outside the framework created by the Arusha Agreement. Accountability for war crimes and crimes against humanity was a major obstacle during the Arusha negotiations and the issue nearly led the talks to collapse. The principal parties to the Agreement, and later the Ceasefire Accords, including CNDD/FDD, had all been implicated in serious war crimes, including the crime of genocide. If the 2005 National Assembly elections had been held strictly within the provisions of the Arusha Agreement, all the prospective candidates, including Pierre Nkurunziza, would have been ineligible for office. The parties, therefore, reached a grand bargain to put aside reconciliation provisions and focus their energies on the power sharing protocols. Fearing the prospect of collapse, mediators relented but nevertheless included a separate provision establishing temporary immunity from prosecution during the transitional period. This immunity however became a defacto permanent amnesty after the transition. It has created a climate where leaders feel that they can get away with serious crimes and this contributes to the kind of human rights violations we have seen since the current crisis erupted in April 2015.

Question. How could the international community better ensure that issues of accountability are not ignored as we implement peace agreements?

Answer. It's important to keep in mind the context in which these peace agreements are being implemented. Post-conflict environments are typically starting from a base of very weak accountability institutions and are subject to constant pushback—and setbacks. (An analysis of democratization transitions over the past two decades, for example, shows that more than half of these efforts experience at least one episode of backsliding). International actors must be prepared for this pushback and be willing to sustain their engagement over time in order to work through difficult periods. (Of those democratic transitions that have had setbacks, two-thirds resume a positive trajectory within three years).

Experience from contexts where accountability structures have emerged from cultures of impunity highlight the importance of establishing multiple layers of accountability rather than relying on a single entity or focal point—which can be more easily circumvented or coopted. Central among these layers are the roles played by the media and civil society organizations. The impetus and persistence in the push for accountability reforms (often a decade or more long process) typically comes from these non-state organizations, particularly until state accountability structures can be created. International actors also have a priority role to play in developing accountability norms in these early stages.

Ensuring space for civil society and media is protected, therefore, is a key priority reducing the likelihood that issues of accountability are ignored in peace agreements. Doing so protects the forums where such sensitive issues can be discussed publicly. Formalizing the role of civil society in fostering accountability in peace agreements can help validate and sustain such civil society engagement. Stipulating that civil society provides an annual assessment of progress on accountability processes is one mechanism for doing this.

While counter-intuitive, international actors can enhance the implementation of accountability objectives of peace agreements by accepting the need to leave a heavier footprint. The responsibilities of external guarantors of peace agreements do not end with the signing of the agreement but must be sustained for the subsequent years until accountability mechanisms are institutionalized. External actors must also be more emboldened to call out spoilers to the implementation of these accountability measures. The tendency is for external partners to defer too quickly to state authorities without recognizing the very nascent levels of state formation often in play. Linking funding support to continued progress in implementing accountability measures can provide further focus to these issues. Incentives for cooperation can also be created with commitments by external partners for increases in funding support when certain accountability thresholds are achieved.

In the case of Burundi, the transitional power-sharing settlement reached by leaders who were themselves implicated in such crimes, was based on the minimum common objective that their ability to secure government office would guarantee temporary immunity. This is one of the weaknesses of the Arusha Accords. None of the leaders at the negotiating table was clean. They put their political differences aside to reach a mutual decision to loosen the Arusha Agreement's accountability provisions. The mediators accepted this because the Agreement was faced with the serious risk of collapsing. This should be a key lesson going forward. If a genuine and inclusive peace process gets underway, the international community should insist on revisiting the issue of accountability as provided for by the Arusha Agreement. Reluctance to accept such accountability measures explains why the CNDD-FDD is currently intent on establishing and driving its own internal peace process.

Question. United Nations Security Council Resolution 1606 adopted in June 2005 calls for the Secretary General to enter into negotiations for a "mixed Truth Commission and a Special Chamber within the court system of Burundi."

What is the status of the establishment of the Commission and the Special Chamber, and how has that impacted political events in Burundi?

What steps have Burundians themselves undertaken to promote reconciliation and healing?

Answer. There has not been progress in establishing the Special Chamber. It was meant to be a support structure embedded inside Burundi's judicial system to provide the competence necessary to handle war crimes and crimes against humanity. These are always difficult issues requiring extremely good capabilities (forensics, anthropology, law, public affairs, research, etc.) It would most likely have been modelled after a similar Chamber that was established in the Uganda High Court.

There was little political will to begin with in the Burundian government to establish a process that it could not control. Accountability for war crimes is an extremely sensitive issue in Burundi because it supports and discredits key political narratives. The hardline Hutu narrative, which is now being revived by the ruling party, stresses the genocide against Hutus in 1972, while the hardline Tutsi narrative, which has been dormant since 2005, stresses the genocide against Tutsis in 1993. Neither narrative accepts its own responsibility for mass atrocities.

The relationship between the Burundian government and the UN hit an all-time low in response to a leaked UN report in July 2014 alleging government recruitment of its youth militia, the Imbonerakure, in preparation for the 2015 elections. This culminated in the closure of the UN Mission in Burundi. These tensions with the UN shut down any prospect that the government would allow the establishment of the Special Chamber. Indeed, the establishment of the Truth and Reconciliation Commission in December 2014 was heavily driven by a desire by the government to hold off international and UN involvement in establishing an accountability framework.

In the absence of political will and leadership and an enabling environment, Burundians have relied on alternative mechanisms of reconciliation and survival. After the Arusha Accords were signed, a strong civil society, comprising hundreds of organizations, developed in Burundi. Private media also played a critical role. Before the May 2015 crackdown on independent media, Burundi was one of the most developed countries in the Great Lakes region from the perspective of independent media and the freedom of expression. This greatly facilitated public discussion on taboo subjects like ethnicity.

Traditional restorative justice practices in which the bashingantahe, or community elders, guide mediation processes between parties in conflict were also commonly employed. These were seen as effective because they were rooted in the local culture and reconciled people at the village level in a relatively inexpensive manner.

Efforts by non-governmental organizations (including initiatives led by the late Howard Wolpe, Search for Common Ground, and Catholic Relief Services) have also been effective. Training across almost 400 peace committees throughout Burundi has facilitated grassroots reconciliation. The peace committee approach has engendered willing participation from all social groups (Hutu, Tutsi and Twa communities).

Indeed, the progress Burundian society has made over the past decade in establishing an inter-ethnic civil society is one of the reasons the current deterioration is so tragic. Notably, depth and cohesiveness of civil society is a key predictor for democratic resiliency and sustaining governance reforms. This holds out hope that if Burundi can avert slipping back into open civil war, the process of recovery could rebound relatively quickly. Along those lines, Burundian women's groups have been in Kampala this week advocating for accountability and reconciliation provisions to be incorporated into the mediation process.

○

www.ingramcontent.com/pod-product-compliance
Lightning Source LLC
Chambersburg PA
CBHW081754280526
45789CB00008B/2850